# SHELL SHOCK
## AND ITS LESSONS

BY

### G. ELLIOT SMITH, M.A., M.D., F.R.C.P., F.R.S.
*Dean of the Faculty of Medicine and Professor of Anatomy
in the University of Manchester*

AND

### T. H. PEAR, B.Sc.
*Lecturer in Experimental Psychology in the University of Manchester*

SECOND EDITION

MANCHESTER
AT THE UNIVERSITY PRESS
12, LIME GROVE, OXFORD ROAD

LONGMANS, GREEN & CO.
LONDON, NEW YORK, BOMBAY, ETC.

1917

PUBLICATIONS OF THE UNIVERSITY OF MANCHESTER

No. CXI.

*First Printed May, 1917*
*Reprinted with slight alterations and a new preface*
*October, 1917*

To
Major R. G. ROWS, M.D., R.A.M.C.

# Contents.

# Preface to First Edition.

OUR reasons for writing this book will be explained by the book itself. We desire here gratefully to acknowledge the help of several friends who have considerably facilitated our task. Our thanks are due to Major R. G. Rows, M.D., R.A.M.C., for his unfailing interest, encouragement and help; to Captains W. H. R. Rivers, M.D., F.R.C.P., F.R.S., and J. W. Astley Cooper of the R.A.M.C., and Mr. E. Gleaves, M.Sc., for their valuable suggestions and assistance in the preparation of the manuscript; to Captain W. E. Sawers Scott, M.D., R.A.M.C., Dr. Albert Hopkinson and Mr. W. Percy Stocks, F.R.C.S., of Manchester, for help in other ways; and to our colleague, Professor H. Bompas Smith, for reading the proofs and helping us to eliminate some of the more glaring literary defects. To the Editor of the *Lancet* we are indebted for permission to use part of an article written by one of us. The stream of requests for fuller information and explanation that poured in upon the author of that article made the writing of this book an unavoidable duty.

G. E. S.
T. H. P.

The Medical School,
The University
Manchester.

*20th April, 1917.*

# Preface to Second Edition.

THE demand for a new edition affords us the opportunity of once more explaining the chief aim of the book, which some of its critics have not adequately understood. Its purpose is to call attention to certain factors in diagnosis and treatment which most physicians have unduly neglected in dealing with incipient mental disturbance. In preparing the book we were not attempting to write a complete manual upon the therapy of mental disease, but were merely pleading for the recognition of the vitally important part played by emotional disturbances in the causation of "shell shock," and the necessity of dealing with those radical causal factors as the basis of really rational and effective treatment.

Those reviewers who have reproved us for neglecting to refer to the usefulness of massage, electricity, baths, *et cetera*, seem to have overlooked the opening paragraph of Chapter II., in which we specifically state that we do not attempt to discuss those general therapeutic measures which every physician is hardly likely to neglect. There is, however, one method of treatment, the use of sedative and soporific drugs, to which we ought to have referred, although it is only recently that the full gravity of the terrible abuse of such methods has been brought home to those who are interested in the welfare of the war-stricken soldier. It cannot be too strongly emphasised that, for the vast majority of the patients suffering from " shell shock," by the time they reach the home hospitals, sedative or sleep-producing drugs are not necessary, and in many cases are positively harmful. A very high proportion of the cases of insomnia in such patients is attributable to worry. The rational means of treatment is to discover the precise nature of the anxieties and worries that are keeping the patient awake and to remove these disturbing influences. The resort to drugs is apt to aggravate the general conditions that induce the continuation of the mental disturbance, and to teach patients, at a time when they are peculiarly susceptible to temptation, the most insidious forms of the drug-habit.

We have been criticised for not having discussed the question of the essential qualifications of nurses in mental hospitals. No one who has had anything to do with the treatment of mentally-afflicted patients, who are often irritable and childishly peevish, is likely to underestimate the vital importance of tact, discretion, and wise firmness on the part of the sisters and nurses. No praise can be too high for those devoted women who achieve success in such trying work. Our book, however, is a plea for the necessity of intimately personal and confidential discussions between patient and doctor, for the purpose of enabling the latter to learn the innermost secrets of the former's individual experience and thereby discover the sources of his distress. These confidences cannot be shared with the nurses, nor indeed with any third person. None of the specific functions and responsibilities of the doctor—and upon these duties it is the chief aim of this book to insist—should be delegated to the nurses.

As our object is to explain the value of psychological analysis and treatment by persuasion, and to insist upon the necessity for the provision of facilities for putting these methods into practice, we have not attempted to describe the mechanisms by means of which emotional disturbances cause the disorganisation of bodily functions. To have dealt in an adequate manner with this fascinating problem and to have discussed the etiology of the interesting cardiac, alimentary and glandular affections would not only have expanded the book to much larger proportions than we desired, but also would have distracted attention from the central principle that we aimed at establishing. We had hoped that the reference (p. 8) to Professor Cannon's suggestive book would have made our readers aware that we were not unmindful of the part played by the sympathetic system, the adrenals and the thyroid glands, in the development of the symptoms of "shell shock," and such particular manifestations of that condition as "soldier's heart,"[1] and "exophthalmic goitre." To have embarked upon such a discussion would have involved a far-reaching excursion into most domains of clinical medicine. We may, however, refer our readers to a recent number of the *Rivista sperimentale di Freniatria* (Vol. 42, F. ii.—iii., 1917), in which Dr. Pighini has given a most illuminating account of the symptoms of "shell shock," and discussed the means by which emotional disturbances can give rise to such far-reaching effects upon the functions of any or every part of the body. He has offered some very interesting suggestions as to the varied rôles played in this process by the central nervous system, the sympathetic system and the thyroid and adrenal glands.

We have received many requests for full reports of cases of "shell shock" and for further information concerning the development of the symptoms, the details of the procedure of psychological analysis, and the utilisation of the evidence obtained from dreams. To have responded to these requests would have added so considerably to the size of the book and so modified its chief character as a plea for reform that we have found it undesirable to comply with them. Hence the book is being re-issued in its original form. We were led to this decision all the more readily since we are aware that a series of small manuals expounding such subjects is now in course of preparation.

---

[1] See Ivy Mackenzie, *Glasgow Medical Journal*, October, 1916.

In this connection we should like to refer those who wish to study a specific example of the usefulness of psychological analysis to the report on "A Case of Claustrophobia," by Captain W. H. R. Rivers, F.R.S., in the *Lancet* of August 18th, 1917, p. 237.

On page 12 we refer to the difficulty of dealing with the many obstinate cases of functional contracture that call for attention. Since that was written Captain E. F. Reeve has suggested a very simple and rational means of curing these troublesome affections, and has demonstrated how conspicuously successful his method of treatment has proved in practice.[1]

His remarks upon the "curative atmosphere" of a successful hospital and the beneficent influence of "psychical infection" provide a corrective to those who assert that the assembling of large numbers of mental patients in one hospital necessarily involves the risk that they will learn undesirable tricks from one another. Experience has shown that, if such patients are properly treated, they also learn from each other how to get well and to cultivate a cheerful mind and a healthy outlook on life.

G. E. S.<br>T. H. P.

THE UNIVERSITY OF MANCHESTER,
    *October, 1917.*

---

[1] "The Treatment of Functional Contracture by Fatigue," *The Lancet*, September 15th, 1917, p. 419.

# Introduction.

SOME account of the reasons for the appearance of this book is due to the reader. During the last year we have been asked repeatedly, both by members of the medical profession and the lay public, to write a simple non-technical exposition of the ascertained facts of that malady, or complex of maladies, for which we have adopted the official designation "shell-shock." Until recently such an attempt would have been premature and largely speculative. But it is now possible to collate the medical reports, not only from our own army, but also from those of France and Russia. Valuable and suggestive data have, furthermore, been obtained from such of the German medical journals as have reached us. The facts described in the various accounts which we have seen are in close agreement. The conclusions in this book, therefore, are not based upon our experience alone.

Our object in thus publishing a brief and simple description of these facts is twofold: first, to make them available to those who have neither the time nor the special knowledge necessary for consultation of the medical journals; secondly, to call attention to the obvious significance of these truths for the future welfare and happiness of the nation.

It might seem that to publish a book on this subject at such a time is merely to irritate existing wounds. The topic is painful; perhaps one of the saddest of the many grievous aspects of the war. But a condition exists at present which is immeasurably more painful—the exaggerated and often unnecessary distress of mind in many of the sufferers and their friends, which arises from the manner in which we, as a nation, have been accustomed to regard even the mildest forms of mental abnormality. Of all varieties of fear, the fear of the unknown is one of the greatest. Not the least of the successful work performed in the special hospitals during the war has been the dispelling of this fear by helping the sufferer to understand his strange symptoms (many of which are merely unusual for the patient himself) and, in the light of this new self-knowledge, to win his own way back to health.

It is because we believe that a similar probing of the *public* wound—the British attitude towards the treatment of mental disorder—though painful, is justifiable and necessary, that we have written the concluding chapters of this book. For it cannot be too strongly urged that the shifting and unstable blend of apathy, superstition, helpless ignorance and fear with which our own country has too long regarded these problems is rapidly becoming our exclusive distinction. It must be realised that America, France, Germany, and Switzerland have long ago faced the problem in the only practical way—the scientific one. And to the long list of sciences which we all agree must be cultivated more assiduously after the war should be added—but not at, or even near, the end—psychiatry, the science of the treatment of mental disorders.

Not patriotic motives alone urge this reform, but common sense and common morality. For shell-shock has brought us no new symptoms. Its sole ground of difference from other disordered states of mind lies in its unusually intense and wide-spreading causes. The problems of shell-shock are the every-day problems of "nervous breakdown." They existed before the war, and they will not disappear miraculously with the coming

of peace. The war has forced upon this country a
rational and humane method of caring for and treating
mental disorder among its soldiers. Are these signs of
progress merely temporary? Are such successful
measures to be limited to the duration of the war, and
to be restricted to the army? Germany has applied them
for years to the alleviation of suffering among her civilian
population, with a success which has made her famous—
outside England. Can we be content to treat our
sufferers with less sympathy, insight and common-sense
than Germany?

It is at this time, while our country is anxiously considering how best to learn the lessons of the war, that
we wish to call attention to one of these lessons which is
in danger of being overlooked.

# CHAPTER I.

## The Nature of Shell-Shock.

A FRENCH doctor has said, "There are no sicknesses, there are only sick people."[1] Whatever may be the general validity of this statement, it is undoubtedly true of the nerve-stricken soldier. Every case is a case by itself, and as such it must be considered by anyone, be he layman or doctor, who is interested in its nature and treatment. For the troubles displayed in the many disorders classed under the official title shell-shock are extraordinarily numerous and different, and their removal necessitates a similarly varied repertoire of "opening moves" on the part of the physician.

Although the term shell-shock has been applied to a group of affections, many of which cannot strictly be designated as "shock," and into the causation of which the effect of the explosion of shells is merely one of many exciting factors, this term has now come to possess a more or less definite significance in official documents and in current conversation. It is for this reason that we have chosen to use it rather than the more satisfactory, but less widely employed term, "War-Strain." The reader will, therefore, understand that whenever the term shell-shock appears in these pages, it is to be understood as a popular but inadequate title for all those mental effects of war experience which are

---

[1] Il n'y a pas de maladies ; il n'y a que des malades.

sufficient to incapacitate a man from the performance
of his military duties. The term is vague; perhaps its
use implies too much; but this is not altogether a disadvantage, for never in the history of mankind have the
stresses and strains laid upon body and mind been so
great or so numerous as in the present war. We may
therefore expect to find many cases which present not a
single disease, not even a mixture, but a chemical compound of diseases, so to speak. In civil life, we often
meet with cases of nervous breakdown uncomplicated
by any gross physical injury. We are scarcely likely,
for example, to meet it complicated by gas poisoning and
a bullet wound. Yet such combinations as these—or
worse—are to be met with in the hospitals every day.

This is perhaps an opportune place to point out a
significant popular misunderstanding concerning the
nature of such maladies as we shall discuss in this
chapter. A common way of describing the condition of
a man sent back with "shock" is to say that he has
"lost his reason" or "lost his senses." As a rule, this
is a singularly inapt description of such a condition.
Whatever may be the state of mind of the patient immediately after the mine explosion, the burial in the
dug-out, the sight and sound of his lacerated comrades,
or other appalling experiences which finally incapacitate
him for service in the firing line, it is true to say that
by the time of his arrival in a hospital in England his
reason and his senses are usually not lost but functioning
with painful efficiency.

His reason tells him quite correctly, and far too often
for his personal comfort, that had he not given, or
failed to carry out, a particular order, certain disastrous
and memory-haunting results might not have happened.
It tells him, quite convincingly, that in his present state
he is not as other men are. Again, the patient reasons,
quite logically, but often from false premises, that since

he is showing certain symptoms which he has always
been taught to associate with "madmen," he is mad
too, or on the way to insanity. If nobody is available
to receive this man's confidence, to knock away the false
foundations of his belief, to bring the whole structure
of his nightmare clattering about his ears, and finally,
to help him to rebuild for himself (not merely to re-
construct for him) a new and enlightened outlook on his
future—in short, if he is left alone, told to "cheer up"
or unwisely isolated, it may be his reason, rather than
the lack of it, which will prove to be his enemy. And
nobody who has observed the hyperæsthesia to noises
and light in the nerve-hospital, nobody who has seen
the effects upon the patients of a coal dropping unexpectedly out of the fire, will have much respect for the
phrase, "lost his senses." There exist, of course, cases
of functional blindness, deafness, cutaneous anæsthesia
and the rest, but the majority of the nerve patients show
none of these disorders and recovery from them is often
rapid.

In a word, it is not in the intellectual but in the
*emotional* sphere that we must look for terms to describe
these conditions. 'These disturbances are characterised
by instability and exaggeration of emotion rather than
by ineffective or impaired reason.[1] And as we shall see
later, in the re-education of the patient, the physician is
compelled continually to take this fact into account.

As we have pointed out, every nerve-stricken soldier
presents a case by itself. Slavish adherence by the
physician to one of the classical names or labels used in
diagnosis usually spells failure. The patient must be
approached *without prejudice*, and the doctor who wishes
to be of real help to him must make up his mind to

---

[1]This subject has been lucidly discussed by C. Burt, "Psychology and the Emotions," *School Hygiene*, May, 1916.

examine and ponder over the sufferer's mental wounds
with as much, nay, even more—care and expenditure of
time than would be given to physical injuries. A mere
cursory inspection in the course of the formal ward visit
is a solemn farce, if it pretends to be a serious attempt
to cure the mentally afflicted.

A man standing at "attention" by the side of his bed,
surrounded by his comrades and faced by the medical
officer, the military sister, and perhaps even by other
members of the staff may volunteer the information that
he is sleeping badly. But this imposing procession and
cloud of witnesses is scarcely conducive to the production
of any further evidence as to the cause of his insomnia.
For of those causes even pre-war experience makes it
possible to assert that their name is legion, and their
character often of an exceedingly intimate and private
nature.

The formal visiting of patients in the wards, while
adequate for the care of physical injuries (which can be
subsequently attended to by trained sisters and nurses)
and necessary for administrative and disciplinary purposes,
is insufficient for "mental cases." It is with this fact in
mind that the military authorities have instituted special
hospitals in which more detailed attention may be given
to the latter class of patients. In these institutions the
soldier may have private interviews with his medical
officer, and the history of the trouble can be unravelled
in conversation. *It is only in this way that any
scientific insight into a case of mental disorder can
be obtained.* A short time spent in such interviews, or even the
perusal, by the uninitiated, of the papers already published in the *Lancet, British Medical Journal*, and elsewhere[1], will convince one of the immense complexity of

---

[1]Such as for instance, D. Forsyth, *Lancet*, Dec. 25th, 1915,

these unusual mental conditions, and moreover, of the absolute necessity of obtaining and understanding the patient's past history, before and during the war. A dozen cases sent back from the front as shell-shock may prove to possess not a single feature in common—except the fact of the shell explosion. And this, as has been pointed out, may be but the "last straw."[1] The patient often discloses in the first interview the fact that he was displaying all his present symptoms *before* the arrival of the particular shell which laid him out.

It is now possible to attempt a brief sketch of the typical conditions which give rise to some of the chief varieties of shell-shock. Let us take a common case; that of the patient who is returned to this country, figuring in the casualty lists under the terse and business-like military formula, "shock, shell."

For various reasons, which the reader will easily supply, we choose to present a composite picture of the history of such a soldier. Not all the conditions described here need necessarily have operated in any one case taken at random, but we shall err, if at all, on the side of understatement. The correctness of the description may be checked by a reference to the papers already mentioned.[2]

We must first try to conceive the experiences of the soldier before the occurrence of the knock-out blow, so far as they bear on his present condition. Let us suppose that his period of training has made him physically and mentally fitter than he had ever been before, that no

---

p. 1399; C. S. Myers, *Lancet*, Mar. 18th, p. 608; R. G. Rows, *Brit. Med. Jour.*, Mar. 25th, 1916, p. 441; G. Elliot Smith, *Lancet*, April 15th and 22nd, 1916; H. Wiltshire, *Lancet*, June 17th, 1916.

[1] Wiltshire, *op. cit.*, p. 1210.

[2] On pp. 4, 5.

military causes of anxiety or fear, such as the experience
or the anticipation of being torpedoed on the outward
voyage, have operated to any noteworthy extent in his
case.    He enters the trenches in first-class condition.
The duration of his stay there, provided he is not
wounded, or attacked by any bodily illness, will depend
from that time forward upon the nature, duration, intensity and frequency of the emotion-exciting causes, and
upon himself.  By that all-inclusive word " himself " we
mean to signify chiefly his temperament, disposition and
character.[1]

It must be remembered that one of the greatest sources
of break-down under such circumstances is intense and
frequently repeated emotion.[2]  By this is meant not only
experiences of fear or of sympathy  with suffering
comrades, in short, those conditions the manifestations
of which might cause the man in the trenches to be
spoken of as " emotional," but also other mental states
associated with general excitement, anxiety, remorse for
major or minor errors, anger, elation, depression and
that complex but very real state, the fear of being afraid.
(The more definite terms of technical psychology are not
used here, as it is considered wiser to employ popular
language.)

The soldier may be subjected to intense emotional
stimuli of this kind for days or weeks without relief. And
whereas to the mental sufferer in civil life sleep often is

---

[1]The reader who is interested in these important distinctions
should consult McDougall, *Social Psychology*, London, 1915,
p. 116.

[2]*Cf.* the statements of two experienced neurologists:—
Déjerine and Gauckler (written before the war), " Overwork
and fatigue are no more a cause of neurasthenia than they are
of tuberculosis.  Without emotion there are no psychoneuroses."

(*The Psychoneuroses and their Treatment by Psychotherapy*, Jelliffe's translation, 1913, p. 232.)

vouchsafed, "setting him on his feet" to continue, more
or less effectively, the struggle next day, to the soldier
sleep may be impossible, not necessarily because of his
excited mental state, but simply from the lack of opportunity or the disturbances going on about him.  In course
of time this loss of sleep from external causes may easilv
set up bodily and mental excitability, which in its turn
acts as a further cause of insomnia.  The usual mental
conditions associated with loss of sleep then rapidly
supervene:  pains and unpleasant organic sensations,
hyperæsthesia, irritability, emotional instability, inability
to fix the attention successfully upon important matters
for any length of time, loss of the power of inhibition and
self-control.[1]

These symptoms, troublesome enough in civil life,
become positively dangerous to the man in the trenches,
especially if he is in a position of responsibility.  In that
case his standing as officer or N.C.O. merely adds to
his mental distress.  Bodily hardship, such as exposure
to cold and wet, hunger, and the irritation from vermin,
obviously aggravates the disorders we have described.

We must not suppose, however, that the man who is
experiencing some or all of these mental and bodily conditions is at this period necessarily displaying any obvious
*outward* signs of his trouble.  There may be no tremor,
no twitchings, no loss of control of the facial or vocal
muscles which would indicate his state even to his neighbours.  He may, for a long time, "consume his own
smoke."  And during this process he may even appear
to his comrades to be steadier and more contemptuous

---

[1] An experimental investigation of the mental effects of loss
of sleep has been carried out by Miss May Smith of the Oxford
Psychological Laboratory.  A short account of these experi-
ments and their results is given in " Some Experimental
Investigations of Fatigue," by T. H. Pear, *Proceedings of
London County Council Conference of Teachers*, 1914.

of danger than before.   Dr. Forsyth[1] has cited some
dramatic incidents, in which officers who imagined that
their instinctive fear was becoming apparent to the men
under their command took unnecessary risks in order to
impress these men with the idea that they were not
afraid.

It must be understood that this suppression of the
external manifestations of an emotion such as fear is but
a partial dominance of the bodily concomitants of that
emotion.   The only changes which can usually be con-
trolled by the will are those of the voluntary or skeletal
muscular system, not those of the involuntary or visceral
mechanism.   While no signs of fear can yet be detected
in the face, the body, limbs or voice, these disturbances
of the respiratory, circulatory, digestive and excretory
systems may be present in a very unpleasant degree,
probably even intensified because the nervous energy
is denied other channels of outlet.[2]

The suppression of fear and other strong emotions is
not demanded only of men in the trenches.   It is constantly expected in ordinary society.   But the experience
of the war has brought two facts prominently before us.
First, before this epoch of trench warfare very few
people have been called upon to suppress fear continually
for a very long period of time.   Secondly, men feel fear
in different ways and in very various degrees.

The first fact accounts for the collapse, under the long
continued strain of trench warfare, of men who have
shown themselves repeatedly to be brave and trustworthy.
They may have felt intense emotions, obviously not of

---

[1] *Op. cit.*, p. 1402.

[2] In his book, "Bodily Changes produced by Fear, Pain,
Hunger and Rage," Professor Cannon has given a striking
demonstration of the importance of emotion in producing
such bodily disturbances.

fear alone, for a long time without displaying any signs of them. But suppression of emotion is a very exhausting process. As Bacon says, "We know diseases of stoppings and suffocations are the most dangerous in the body; and it is not much otherwise in the mind."

The second fact mentioned above is of great importance in the consideration of our problem. There are undoubtedly men who seem to be immune to fear of the dangers of warfare. But to them we can scarcely apply the adjective "brave." The brave man is one, who, feeling fear, either overcomes it or refuses to allow its effects to prevent the execution of his duty.

Other emotional states however, besides fear, arise and require suppression. The tendency to feel sympathetic pain or distress at harrowing sights and sounds, disgust or nausea at the happenings in the trenches, the "jumpy" tension in face of unknown dangers such as mines—all these, like fear, are or have been biologically useful under natural conditions and, like it, are deeply and innately rooted in man. But the unnatural conditions of modern warfare make it necessary that they shall be held in check for extraordinarily long periods of time.

The impossibility of regarding modern methods of warfare in the same light as natural and primitive means of fighting appears very clearly when we consider the instinctive and emotional factors involved in the two sets of circumstances. In natural fighting, face to face with his antagonist, and armed only with his hands or with some primitive weapon for close fighting, the uppermost instinct in a healthy man would naturally be that of pugnacity, with its accompanying emotion of anger. The effect of every blow would be visible, and the intense excitement aroused in the relatively short contest would tend to obliterate the action of other instincts such as that of flight, with its emotion of fear. But in trench

warfare the conditions are different. A man has seldom
a personal enemy whom he can see and upon whom he
can observe the effects of his attacks. His anger cannot
be directed intensely night and day against a trench
full of unseen men in the same way in which it can be
provoked by an attack upon him by an individual. And
frequently the assaults made upon him nowadays are
impersonal, undiscriminating and unpredictable, as in the
case of heavy shelling. One natural way is forbidden
him in which he might give vent to his pent-up emotion,
by rushing out and charging the enemy. He is thus
attacked from within and without. The noise of the
bursting shells, the premonitory sounds of approaching
missiles during exciting periods of waiting, and the sight
of those injured in his vicinity whom he cannot help,
all assail him, while at the same time he may be fighting
desperately with himself. Finally, he may collapse when
a shell bursts near him, though he need not necessarily
have been injured by actual contact with particles of the
bursting missile, earth thrown up by its impact, or gases
emanating from its explosion. He may or may not be
rendered unconscious at the time.[1] He is removed from
the trenches with loss of consciousness or in a dazed or
delirious condition with twitchings, tremblings or absence
of muscular power.

Upon recovery of consciousness, which may take place
after periods varying between a few minutes and a few
weeks, the immediate disorders of sensation, emotion,
intellect, and movement, are often very severe. It may

---

[1]Capt. Wiltshire, as a result of recent experience near the
firing line in France thinks that the men's accounts of the
duration of unconsciousness are often exaggerated, owing to
their faulty memory of the time at which it occurred. He also
says that in his opinion the actual individual shell-shock which
prostrates the man is but the final precipitating cause. (*Op.
cit.*, p. 1207.)

be presumed that at the beginning of the war they must have appeared far more serious to most of the doctors who saw them in their early stages than they would now. This speculation is suggested by the evidence of the case-sheets sent with the men from France in the early period of the campaign. Such diagnoses as "delusional insanity," and other similar terms taken from the current classifications of advanced conditions of insanity, appear very frequently as descriptions of cases which on arrival in England had almost entirely lost every sign of mental unusualness. In fact, one of the most cheering aspects of work amongst this type of case has been the rapidity with which men who have presented quite alarming symptoms have subsequently recovered.

It may seem almost unnecessary to enumerate the bizarre phenomena which constitute the immediate results of shell-shock, for our newspapers have naturally seized upon such unusual details and have made the most of their opportunities in this direction. But the reader will obtain a clearer idea of the facts if they are catalogued once more.

The most obvious phenomena are undoubtedly the disturbances of sensation and movement. A soldier may be struck blind, deaf or dumb by a bursting shell: in rare cases he may exhibit all three disorders simultaneously or even successively. It should be added that these troubles often vanish after a short space of time, as suddenly and dramatically as they appeared. Thus one of the blinded soldier survivors of the *Hesperian* recovered his sight on being thrown into the water. Other blind patients have had their sight restored under the action of hypnosis. Mutism is often conquered by the shock of a violent emotion, produced accidentally or purposely. Examples of such "shocking" events taken at random from our experience were the sight of another patient slipping from the arms of an orderly, the "going

under " chloroform, the application of a faradic current
to the neck, the announcement at a " picture house " of
Rumania's entry into the war (this cured two cases
simultaneously), and the sight of the antics of our most
popular film comedian.  The latter agency cured a case
of functional deaf-mutism, the patient's first auditory
sensations being the sound of his own laugh.

The muscular system may be affected in an equally
striking manner.  Contractures often occur in which a
man's fist may be immovably clenched for months; or
his back may be bent almost at right angles to his
lower limbs, there being in neither case any bodily change
discoverable by the neurologist which can account for
such a condition.  These contractures, though curable,
often prove very obstinate, and at present their nature
remains somewhat of a mystery.[1]  Other distressing and
long continued disturbances take the form of muscular
twitchings and tremors or loss of power in the limbs.

Not every nerve-case, however, presents such striking
and objective signs as those which we have just been
describing.  The *subjective* disturbances, which are apt
to go undiscovered in a cursory examination of the
patient, are frequently more serious than the objective,[2]
and are experienced by thousands of patients who to the
mere casual observer may present no more signs of
abnormality than a slight tremor, a stammer, or a depressed or excited expression.  These afflictions: loss of
memory, insomnia, terrifying dreams, pains, emotional
instability, diminution of self-confidence and self-control,
attacks of unconsciousness or of changed consciousness
sometimes accompanied by convulsive movements resembling those characteristic of epileptic fits, incapacity to

[1] See, however, Preface to Second Edition, p. viii.

[2] This fact is in danger of being overlooked by members of
the public whose knowledge of " shock " is obtained from the
newspaper reports.

understand any but the simplest matters, obsessive
thoughts, usually of the gloomiest and most painful kind,
even in some cases hallucinations and incipient delusions
—make life for some of their victims a veritable hell.
Such patients may have recovered from sensory or motor
disturbances and yet may suffer from any or all of
these afflictions as a residuum from the original " shock-
complex; " they may suffer from them as a complication
of the discomfort attending upon a wound or an illness,
or, on the other hand, they may have no overt bodily
disorder: their malady then being usually given the simple
but all-inclusive (and blessed) description " neurasthenia."

Now the happiness and welfare of such men obviously
is bound up to no small extent with the character of the
hospital or hospitals (for the plural number is commonly
to be used in writing the history of these patients) to
which they are sent.   In the general military hospitals
the medical officers have neither the time nor, in many
cases, the special knowledge, necessary to deal with cases
of this kind.   Such patients may recover of themselves
without any treatment, but a large number of them tend
to get worse, and if they are left without attention their
symptoms are apt to become stereotyped into definite
delusions and hallucinations.   Moreover, in a general
ward such men may become a constant source of disturbance and annoyance to other patients and to the
nurses.   One of the symptoms of their illness is a morbid
irritability;   they tend to become upset and to take
offence at the merest trifles[1]—and this leads to trouble
with patients, nurses, and the medical officers responsible
for discipline.   But if special consideration is shown
them by the nurses the other patients are apt to mis-
understand it and even to complain of favouritism.   In
other words, when mixed with wound-cases in a general

---

[1] R. G. Rows, *op. cit.*, p. 441.

hospital, these nervous patients are apt to be regarded as a nuisance—which is bad for them and for the proper working of the hospital. Another consideration, too, is that the subjection of such men to irksome regulations of military discipline, and the usual penalties for infringing them, is often so potent a factor in producing disturbances as to be quite fatal to any hope of amelioration.

These considerations have led the military authorities to establish special hospitals for nerve-cases.[1] In such institutions the patients can be nursed and attended to by a staff which, being used to the idiosyncrasies of such illnesses can make conditions more suitable to them.

A man's particular nervous malady is likely to be of common occurrence in the nerve-hospital; it does not render him conspicuous, and therefore an object of fussy solicitude, galling pity, or suspicious contempt, as is too often the case in other institutions. If unwounded, he need not suffer the taunt of "having nothing to show" as his reason for staying in hospital. Further, while in the special hospital, more importance is attached to some of the patient's symptoms, less disturbance is produced by others. The occurrence of a "fit" is viewed by the rest of the men in this class of hospital in a truer perspective, and the patient does not find himself a nine-days' wonder, as he so easily may do in a small

---

[1]For particulars of these hospitals, see W. Aldren Turner's Report, *Lancet*, May 27th, 1916, p. 1073. The reports published in the special war numbers of the *Revue Neurologique* (and especially Nos. 23, 24, November and December, 1915) bear ample testimony to the magnificent work being done by the French in this direction. Not only has special provision been made in each military district for dealing with neurological and mental cases, but also admirable accounts of the work are being published, and those responsible for the care of such patients have been afforded many opportunities for discussing their difficulties and learning from each other.

auxiliary hospital full of straightforward wound cases.

Up to this point we have discussed the various troubles subsumed under the term shell-shock in what may be termed its initial and middle stages. In the middle stage, the patient having recovered from the severe and acute symptoms constituting the former phase, is left with a motley residuum of troubles, the chief of which we have enumerated on pages 12, 13. In distinguishing between this middle stage and that which follows it, we may perhaps ask the reader to assist us by recalling the difference between a mechanical mixture and a chemical compound. In the former the ingredients of the mixture remain unaltered and unaffected by the proximity of other substances, as for example when sugar is mixed with sand. In the compound, on the other hand, chemical action and reaction occur between the components so that not one of the substances is immediately recognisable in the complex, as for example when carbon, hydrogen and oxygen combine to form alcohol, which resembles none of them.

Now it would be distorting the facts of mind to suggest that while the third stage of shell-shock is a compound (as it undoubtedly is) the middle stage is a mixture. For the very essence of mind is its compound nature. But what we wish to point out is that in this middle stage the abnormalities have had very little time to react upon each other, with the result that there is some resemblance to a state of mixture, the phenomena existing temporarily side by side, so to speak. In this stage a patient may be troubled simultaneously by several unusual mental occurrences, such as terrifying dreams during very light sleep, loss of memory for certain periods of his past, and inability to understand or to carry out complex orders. For a short time in his " bowled-over " state he may be worried by the separate attacks, of these various troubles at different periods of the day and he may be too overwhelmed to try to understand

or to attempt to see relations between them.   This state
of mind, in which the patient is still his "old self,"
though a somewhat overturned self, resembles the
mechanical mixture in our illustration.   The reader may
obtain some idea of this condition if he recalls any one
day in his own experience when "everything seemed to
go wrong"; when at one moment he was turning to
face this difficulty, at another, that, but still retained to
a great extent his usual attitude towards the world.

As has been pointed out, however, the state of
"mechanical mixture" is utterly alien to the normal
mind, which tends rapidly to interpret, in the light of
its own experience, and to integrate as far as possible,
its events, however incongruous they may be.   The mind
cannot, for any length of time, allow a new experience
to remain strange or undigested.   It must gather in and
assimilate that event to the systematised complex which
we call its own past experience.   It follows that the
ultimate result upon any particular mind of a new experience, if it be of a personally significant nature, will
depend almost entirely upon the past history of that
mind.

Thus for example the question whether the patient
can or cannot satisfactorily stand up to his new troubles
will be determined not only by his disposition, temperament and character, but also by his previous personal
experience.

It is thus obvious to anyone who gives the matter
any serious consideration, that the manifestation of a
severe psychical shock must necessarily be determined
in a large measure by the nature of the mind upon which
the injury falls.   It would be idle to pretend therefore,
that, in diagnosis, the story of the patient's past experience can be left out of account, for the manifestation
of the injury will obviously depend largely upon the
individual patient's "mental make-up."

Faced by the existence of a number of unusual mental phenomena the patient will inevitably succeed in time in inventing for himself, explanations of their co-existence. This "rationalisation,"[1] as it is called, is a perfectly normal process which is constantly going on in every individual, yet it plays a great part in complicating the mental disorders of the middle stage, and thereby intensifying the patient's ultimate distress. For instance, he may not be more than temporarily disturbed by the unusual experiences we have mentioned[2] if they assail him separately. But, given time, he will soon begin to connect their appearances, and will argue to himself that these phenomena can have only one meaning: that he is mad or rapidly becoming so. And in this completely erroneous procedure he will be aided and abetted, not only by his own ignorance of the relation of mental normality to abnormality, but also by the general tendency of the uneducated to class everything unusual in the mental sphere as "mad." Once he is convinced that he is in this state he may easily lose all hope of getting better, thereby increasing enormously the gravity of his case. Completely illogical, but to him entirely satisfactory explanations of his condition will then multiply.

As we have mentioned, this rationalisation is no unusual phenomenon in ordinary life. It will be clear to anyone who gives the question a moment's thought that few of the non-scientific[3] beliefs held by even a highly educated person have ever been logically reasoned out from fundamental principles. In fact such principles

---

[1] Or "seeking conscious and rational grounds for actions" (and beliefs) "whose motives are largely unconscious and perhaps irrational." (A description borrowed from Burt's article, *q. v.*)

[2] On pp. 12, 13.

[3] (and, obviously, the same may be said of not a few 'scientific' beliefs.)

frequently cannot be reached, for the very good reason that they have never been consciously conceived by the individual. One's views on religion, politics, or the relations and rights of the sexes may exhibit in their outer casings a semblance of rational structure: their core, however, is not reason but emotion. As James expresses it:—

> "In its inner nature, belief or the sense of reality is a sort of feeling more allied to the emotions than to anything else . . . reality means simply relation to our emotional and active life. This is the only sense which the word ever has in the mouths of practical men. . . Whenever an object so appeals to us that we turn to it, accept it, fill our mind with it, or practically take account of it, so far it is real for us and we believe it. Whenever, on the contrary, we ignore it, fail to consider it or act upon it, despise it, reject it, forget it, so far it is unreal for us and is disbelieved. . . . Whatever things have intimate and continuous connection with my life are things whose reality I cannot doubt."[1]

Few people, however, realise this truth so clearly, or express it so lucidly, as Professor James. Often we believe that we are logically convinced when in reality we have been convinced first, and have invented reasons for our conviction afterwards. But many of our beliefs and attitudes have been implanted in us in childhood or early youth by processes which could not by the wildest stretch of imagination be called logical. And not the least important of those beliefs are those held by the average Briton with regard to insanity.[2]

For the patient, then, his mental troubles, having intimate and continuous connection with his life, become very real indeed. But the longer he is left alone to "cheer up," the longer he broods over his

---

[1] *Principles of Psychology*, II., 283-324.

[2] The opinions of Dr. Bedford Pierce upon this matter are highly important. *British Medical Journal*, January 8th, 1916, p. 4.

troubles in isolation, the longer he is allowed to build theories upon his inadequate and inaccurate data, the more intimately and continuously connected with his life will the abnormalities become. They may come to be so integrated with each other that his very personality becomes tinged. Then he is no longer a normal person battling with his separate enemies, but one who has made terms, and those often disastrous ones, with his closely allied foes. An attempt to cure him at this stage will then necessitate the analysis of a highly complex compound, while in the early and middle stages merely the attack upon separated elements is necessary.

We are concerned at present with the facts of shell-shock, but this is perhaps a suitable place in which to deal with an opinion about this set of phenomena, which is not uncommon, especially perhaps in people above military age. That judgment, expressed sometimes bluntly, but oftener in a more subtle fashion, is that shock or neurasthenia are polite names for nothing else but "funk." It is not easy to take a dispassionate view of this question, but to persons holding this opinion the following points are worthy of consideration.

First, the most severe and distressing symptoms occur to a surprising extent in the case of those patients whose past history shows that, far from possessing even the normal quota of timidity, they had been noted for their "dare-devilry" and had been specially chosen as despatch-riders, snipers and stretcher-bearers in the firing line. Secondly, it is not uncommon for patients to ask to be sent back to duty because they feel that they have been too long with nothing to do, while it is quite obvious to the doctor that they are as yet unfit to bear any great strain. Thirdly, the seasoned regular, officer or N.C.O.,[1]

---

[1]Our personal experience has been of privates and non-commissioned officers only, but there is no *a priori* reason for

as well as the young soldier of only a few months' service may display precisely the same symptoms as those we have described. Such men have frequently been in the army for many years, and have fought on previous occasions with great success. Their strength of mind and body has been demonstrated over and over again, yet at last they have broken down. And they manifest the greatest concern at their unusual symptoms.

It will be readily granted, of course, that there exist among the nerve patients returned from the front cases in which there is genuine fear of the war, arising from memories of the experiences which they have undergone. Even this state of mind, however, is usually expressed by the patient in some such phrase as " I don't want to go back, but I'll go quite willingly if I'm ordered to." It should not be forgotten, moreover, that not a small number of instances are known in which these men prove to have made repeated attempts at enlistment after having been rejected several times, or even discharged from the army, changing their medical examiner until they have succeeded. One case, presenting a great number of the symptoms of shell-shock in a very intense form, including, beside the ordinary neurasthenic troubles, blindness, deafness, and mutism at successive times, was that of a man who had been discharged from the army as medically unfit and had re-enlisted.

Two cases may be quoted here in illustration of some of these assertions:

The first is that of a non-commissioned officer who went through the initial eleven months of the war in France and Flanders, was subjected to every kind of strain, physical, mental and moral, which that stricken

supposing that these remarks do not apply to the commissioned ranks. It has been found that in the French Army the cases of neurasthenia amongst officers have been very numerous.

field provided; and in addition was wounded twice, gassed twice, and buried under a house, on all five occasions being treated in the field ambulance and then returning to the trenches. After all this experience he had not qualified for sick leave, but was granted five days ordinary leave to return home, apparently in a good state of health. After reaching England and while waiting for a train in the railway station, he suddenly collapsed, became unconscious, and for months afterwards was the subject of severe neurasthenia. Apparently at the front the excitement, the sense of responsibility and especially the example that he felt he should set his men, seem to have kept him right. These stimuli removed, he broke down. The whole of his trouble seemed to be due to the dread lest on his return to the front, the added responsibilities which would fall upon his shoulders (because most of his own officers had been killed and there would be new men to replace them) might be too much for him. His intelligence seemed (to himself) to have become numbed by his experiences, and he became conscious of the unreliability of his memory and of his inability to understand not only complex orders, but, as he put it, "even the newspapers." It was this that excited in him the dread lest he should be incompetent to discharge adequately the duties which would fall upon him. There was nothing of malingering or shirking in his case. There was no fear of physical injuries or of returning to the front; on the contrary, he was anxious to go back. His fear lest the possibility of his failure would be bad for his platoon was wholly due to that admirable sentiment of regimental loyalty, which comes out so strikingly in the nervous troubles of the non-commissioned officer.

This class of case demands a great deal of patient and sympathetic attention before the real cause of the trouble is elicited, and then months of re-education may be required to build up anew the man's confidence in himself.

The second case is that of a soldier who had suffered from severe shock symptoms and had recovered. In conversation with the medical officer the soldier expressed his willingness, and even his desire, to return to the front, in full knowledge of the fact that the officer's report in that sense would lead to his being sent back to fight. That night the patient was awakened by a terrifying dream, the true significance of which was certainly not adequately appreciated by him. Although he dreamt that he was afraid to go back to the front, apparently he did not realise that he was actually afraid—*i.e.*, that the dream had any meaning. On examination it proved to be a detailed forecast of the imaginary incidents of his return to his regiment, and of his attempt to commit suicide when ordered to go to France. Here was a man who of his own initiative had asked his doctor to certify him as ready to go back, yet in his sleep the train of thought, started by the discussion of the possibility of his return, working subconsciously, had stirred up images of what this implied, and reinstated emotions of so terrifying a nature that in his dream he preferred suicide to facing the ordeal again.

It may perhaps be allowable to quote in this connection the view of a German neurologist, Prof. Gaupp, on the "shock-cases" which have been sent back from the German front.[1] At the same time it is important to remind our readers that Gaupp is writing of a conscript army, the authorities in which are certainly not notorious for lenity to the individual; further, that up to the time of writing the present chapter, all the "shock" patients in Great Britain have been men who voluntarily elected to serve their country, the majority of

---

[1] "Hysterie und Kriegsdienst" (Hysteria and War Service), *Münchener Medizinische Wochenschrift*, March 16th, 1915.

them having enlisted in the earliest stages of the war.

In discussing cases where nervous trouble, uncontrollable in nature and intensity, had led to the patients being kept in German hospitals for months, it was sometimes found that the mental foundation which was a causal factor of these troubles was a more or less conscious anxiety concerning the possibility of a return to the front.

"There is no justification," says Gaupp, "for calling every instance of this a case of malingering or simulation. There are quite capable men of irreproachable character whose nervous system is positively unfitted for the hardships and horrors of war. They have enthusiasm and the best of intentions but these cease to inspire them when the horrors and terrors come. Their inner strength rapidly decreases, and it only requires an acute storm to break upon the nervous system (such as the explosion of a shell or the death of comrades) for their self-control to vanish completely. Then automatically their condition changes into what is popularly called ' hysteria.' The exhausted mind then feels that it is no longer master of the situation, and therefore ' takes refuge in disease.' At first, as a rule, obvious signs of terror and anxiety (trembling, twitching, etc.) manifest themselves; if these are cured there still remain chronic symptoms of hypochondria and despondency. Time, however, has its effect in many of these cases."[1]

If a patient comes into the hands of a physician before the processes of rationalisation and systematisation have become established, the medical officer should be able to meet his difficulties, and help him correctly to interpret his unusual experiences by explaining to him their origin and nature.

" The application of discreet sympathy and tact by a physician who endeavours to discover something of the man's past mental history may be able to reassure a patient upon his particular trouble with the happiest of results. To a man quite

---

[1] The translation is very free, but it fairly represents the sense of the German original.

unacquainted with text-books or speculation on psychology there can be no darker mystery than the working of other people's minds. To such a man the natural conclusion is that his own mental processes are universal and normal. But if, as a result of some nerve-shattering experience of warfare his mind suddenly develops a trick which was quite unknown to him before, though this development may be far from abnormal, to the troubled patient it may seem to be an unquestionable symptom of madness." [1]

Many of the cases in which a patient has merely needed reassuring have been of this type. A short and very simple explanation of some elementary facts of psychology is often sufficient to bring about an immense change in the man's condition, which has led to his curing himself. And this is the ideal method of cure.

It may seem that an inordinate amount of space has been devoted to the demonstration of a simple truth, that mental, like bodily disorder, should be treated early, or complications may ensue. But there are reasons for giving so much prominence to this aspect of the subject. The chief is that in our own country, mental disorder is seldom treated in its early stages. Nearly all our elaborate public machinery for dealing with this distressing form of illness is devised, and in practice is available, only for the advanced cases. This war has shown clearly a truth which, of course, was already known before to many doctors, but never adequately appreciated by the general public, that a case of advanced mental disorder may pass not only through various milder stages on its way, but that if intercepted at these earlier stages, it may frequently be cured with ease.

Another point which should be emphasised is this: shell-shock involves no *new* symptoms or disorders,

[1] From a leading article on " War-Shock and its Treatment," in the *Manchester Guardian*.

Every one was known beforehand in civil life. If by any stretch of the imagination we could speak of a specific variety of disease called shell-shock, it would be new only in its unusually great number of ingredients. And the most gratifying truth of all is that even this hydra-headed monster, if caught young, can be destroyed.

From the fact that shell-shock includes no new disorders the important inference may be drawn that the medical lessons taught by the war must not be forgotten when peace comes. The civilian should be offered the facilities for cure which have proved such a blessing to the war-stricken soldier.

# CHAPTER II.

# Treatment.

IN discussing the question of treatment we do not
propose to deal with general therapeutic measures
which every physician in charge of nervous or mental
patients is hardly likely to neglect.[1] The importance of
a generous and easily digested dietary is generally recognised: as also is the need for quiet and congenial
surroundings, and for shielding patients from disturbances, such as noises and the sight of wounded, which
are likely to evoke painful emotions and vivid memories
of their experiences at the front. It is also obviously
important that the physician should deal promptly and
discreetly with any bodily ailments from which the patient
is suffering, being careful neither to minimise their gravity
and so give him any reason for the grievance that he
is not receiving proper attention, nor by exaggerating
them to add this anxiety to his other troubles.[2] These
are questions which may confidently be left to the discretion of the physician in charge.

---

[1]Such, for example, as those set forth in the series of
articles in Vol. VIII, of Sir Clifford Allbutt's *System of
Medicine*, 1899, pp. 88-233.

[2]The part played by bodily disease in the causation of
mental disturbance has been concisely summarised by Sir
G. H. Savage in the introductory chapter on Mental Disease
in Vol. VIII. of Allbutt's *System of Medicine*, pp. 191-195.

*Firmness and Sympathy.*

But there are certain other therapeutic measures commonly recommended in text-books for application in the
cases of patients suffering from neurasthenic and hysterical
troubles, which cannot be thus summarily dismissed. As
many of these patients are irritable and childishly peevish,
it is necessary that they should be treated with sympathetic firmness, tact and insight. But, unfortunately,
the words "firmness" and "sympathy" are interpreted
in a great variety of ways. While it is important, for
purely therapeutic reasons, that discipline should be
maintained, and that when the physician has decided
what he considers the proper treatment for the patient
this should be rigorously carried out, it is manifestly
disturbing and injurious in many cases for the officer
to insist upon all the exacting details of military rules
and regulations. For the mentally healthy soldier,
obedience to stern and even harshly rigid regulations is
often vitally important; but an attempt by a medical
officer to treat a ward of neurasthenic patients in this way
usually has disastrous results.

Quite apart, however, from the military aspects of the
case, the physician, without really investigating the history
of a patient, may label his trouble "hysteria" and forthwith adopt a course of "firmness." He may assume
the attitude of doubting the genuineness of symptoms
which are very real to the sufferer. Under the plea of
helping to cure the patient the officer may assure him
that there is nothing much the matter with him and that
if he tries he will soon be all right. Such advice may
be justifiable if based on a real insight into the state
of the individual sufferer, but this knowledge can be
gained only by a patient investigation of the cause of
his trouble. If the advice is given without this insight, it
is a mere shot in the dark. The fact that the device
succeeds in a certain number of cases is no excuse for its

general adoption. And when it "misfires" no one realises the fact more quickly than the patient himself. He realises that the officer does not appreciate his condition and his confidence is thereby destroyed.

It is useful, too, to consider for a moment the nature of treatment by "sympathy." When we used the phrase "sympathetic firmness" we intended to indicate the insistence upon a strict observance of such methods of treatment as a real insight into the patient's condition may suggest. The word "sympathy" was used in its literal sense of "feeling with" the sufferer. But there is no class of patients upon whom sympathy of the injudicious kind is more prone to work serious harm than the psychoneurotic. The knowledge of this fact is often the excuse for the adoption of the opposite attitude and the prescription of "firmness" which, as we have seen, may be equally unintelligent and injudicious.

But sympathy of the injudicious kind is not *real* sympathy. For unless the sympathiser has a true appreciation of the patient's condition, and can look at things from his point of view, he cannot really feel *with* the sufferer. The latter may arouse in the would-be sympathiser tender emotions and sympathetic " pain," but unless the sympathiser have insight, the pain, to put it crudely, is not likely to be "in the same place" as that of the patient. Such misplaced emotion and false sympathy, whether on the part of the doctor, the nurse, or the patient's relations, may do much harm.

In mild cases of mental trouble, however, where the patient still retains a goodly portion of self-confidence and self-respect, this "petting" variety of sympathy may sometimes be effective. Such a patient may be cheered up by the presence of people sufficiently interested in him to be sorry for his condition; and it may help him to look on the brighter side of things and to forget his worries and anxieties. But often it is apt, by suggestion,

to aggravate his troubles or even to discourage him from
trying to recover.[1]　Perhaps it would be more accurate
to say that such treatment gives him no inducement to
get better.

There are still not a few physicians who regard the
group of functional troubles commonly labelled "hysteria" as something closely akin to malingering.　If it
would not be considered invidious we could quote the
opinions of well-known physicians published within the
last five years, suggesting that there is no real line of
demarcation.　(It is not uncommon to meet the expression "*detecting*," instead of *diagnosing* hysteria.)

But even among those who regard these serious affections as something more than mere simulation there is a
tendency to look upon any form of sympathy as a dangerous pandering to the patient's lack of will power.[2]

This attitude often finds expression in leaving the patient
alone to get better by his own efforts, or in suggesting to
him that he is not so ill as he thinks he is, and that all
he needs is some work to occupy his attention.

The attempt is often made to justify such methods by
the plea that it is "bad for the patient to talk to him of
his worries."　But how a physician is to rid a patient
of the very root of all his trouble without first discovering
and then discussing it with him is not apparent.　Nor,
again, is it any more rational merely to tell a man who is
weighed down with some very real anxiety to "cheer up,"
or to "work in the garden," or "take a walking tour."

We are not maintaining that such methods do not
often meet with success in the case of many patients who

---

[1] Or in some mild cases, to encourage him to wish to
remain an invalid under such pleasant conditions.

[2] In his careful studies of these conditions, C. S. Myers
has called attention to the mistaken notion of regarding these
troubles as "fundamentally due to disordered volition," *Lancet*,
Sept. 9th, 1916, p. 467.

are only mildly affected and earnestly want to get better.
But experience shows that such advice is often fraught
with danger, and, in severe cases of mental affection is
worse than useless. The experience of those physicians
who have been treating such patients with sympathetic
insight during the last two years affords a striking condemnation of the theory that it is generally "bad to talk
to them of their worries." It has repeatedly happened
that as soon as the patient was asked about his troubles
he made a full statement of all that was troubling him
and was obviously relieved to confess his worries to
someone who took an intelligent interest in his welfare.

In many cases the mere unburdening of this weight
of anxiety and the removal by the physician of quite
trivial misunderstandings which were the original causes
of it, were sufficient to cheer up the patient and to start
him on the way to complete recovery. Yet many of
these men had been inmates of a series of hospitals in
which no attempt had been made to discover what was
the real source of all the trouble. Thus to their other
worries and anxieties was added the real additional
grievance that they were being neglected and were of
no account. In many cases this constituted a serious
aggravation of the patient's mental disturbance and
encouraged him to believe that his state was already
beyond help.

Those physicians who look upon such milder psychoses
as varieties of simulation should be reminded that the
methods we have just mentioned are not often likely to
be effective in cases of real malingering.

In discussing the therapeutic use of "firmness" we
have not thought it necessary to mention those applica-
tions of this method which at times are practised by
combatant officers at the front. The use of military
authority to suppress the minor manifestations of nervous-
ness, or the resort to such expedients as unexpectedly

firing off a gun alongside a man afflicted with functional deafness, are merely examples of the application of "suggestion." They are akin to the use of "firmness" by the physician who has not investigated the cause of the patient's trouble. The results of such expedients are as erratic in the one case as in the other. But there is no need for us to discuss this practice further, except to add that the knowledge that such "treatment by military authority" has been tried before, still further diminishes the justification for resorting to such measures when the patient reaches the home hospital.

*Isolation.* Many physicians regard isolation as an appropriate method of treatment for soldiers suffering from shock, and they urge in justification of such a procedure the success which often attends its use in civil cases. We do not deny the utility of isolation for suitable cases, and success has attended its use when the patient's condition obviously required it. But the circumstances which were responsible for causing the mental disturbance in the soldier may be of a totally different nature from those which have upset the civilian; and therapeutic measures which may be appropriate in eliminating the civilian's sources of irritation might be wholly unsuitable, if not positively harmful, in the case of soldiers.

It cannot be too strongly emphasised in connection with this subject that most of the theory and practice of treating hysteria by isolation has been developed in civil life, and in very many cases with reference to well-to-do women living in the lap of luxury. When such persons develop hysterical symptoms, some sources of irritation in the home or the social environment are often responsible. By isolation the patient is removed from the noxious influence of both domestic worries and mistaken sympathy; his or her whims and fancies are compulsorily subordinated by self-discipline and con-

sideration for others. At home it is impossible satisfactorily to enforce such measures and the attempt to
do so will almost inevitably fail, because sympathy,
curiosity and anxiety on the part of various relatives
hinder the attainment of these objects. By isolation the
patient is removed from these unfavourable psychical
influences. Through the freedom from such disturbing
stimuli, the abnormally intense reaction of the mind is
reduced. And in many patients of this class the desire
to be cured or to be active, which is produced by the
boredom of isolation, works favourably.[1]

But in most soldiers the circumstances are altogether
different. In the first place, the patient secures the
change of surroundings by his removal from the
trenches to the hospital. Isolation, therefore, can hardly
be justified on that score. At the same time, the
removal to a military hospital at any rate should obviate
all danger of his being pestered by foolish relatives and
friends with their mistaken sympathy or excessive attention. And as regards the importance of discipline and
routine, the soldier is in a position very different from
that of the wealthy society lady, for he has already been
subjected to such training.

In some instances, however, just as in the civil cases,
the boredom of isolation may produce the good effects
noted above. But there is the corresponding disadvantage
that if you isolate a man and put a special nurse to look
after him it is impossible to convince him that his case
is not serious. It may, indeed, help him to persuade
himself that he is really going insane. As a matter of
experience, it is found that very many men cannot stand
isolation for long; they feel that they must break out,
even if they realise that punishment is certain for doing

---

[1]This explanation of the reasons for the use of isolation is taken
from Mohr's article in Lewandowsky's *Handbuch der Neurologie*

so. The conversation of patients who are undergoing treatment by isolation is often perfectly frank about it. They tell the medical officer they will break out at the first opportunity; that the few hours of freedom would more than compensate for the punishment which would come afterwards. Again, it must be apparent that, when the trouble is due in any considerable measure to the re-awakening of emotions linked up with some painful earlier experience, isolation is not likely to be effective in many cases, and may be definitely harmful. Neither should it be forgotten that such measures fail to isolate the patient from his worst enemy, himself.

Even in those cases in which it is useful, isolation, if unduly prolonged, may spoil its own good effects. It may so accustom the patient to a solitary mode of existence that the presence of other persons may make him irritable when at the end of his time of seclusion he is compelled to associate with his fellows.

There is another fact which has to be taken into consideration—and this applies especially in civil practice, where the patient or his family have to pay for the treatment. We refer to the expensiveness of treatment by isolation. Unless it can be shown that it is the best or the only hopeful method to adopt, the physician must feel some hesitancy in the majority of cases, in prescribing such costly measures.[1]

Déjerine and Gauckler[2] have given an admirable account of the use of isolation in the treatment of neurasthenia and hysteria. They are careful to point out, however, that even in the case of civilian patients, with whom of course their treatise is concerned, "iso-

---

[1] As Sir Clifford Allbutt has pointed out (*op. cit.*, p. 158).

[2] *The Psychoneuroses and their Treatment by Psychotherapy*, translated from the French by Jelliffe, 2nd Edition, 1913, p. 311.

lation, even accompanied by rest and overfeeding, is never enough." It is merely an adjunct, though, under certain circumstances, a necessary one, of the treatment by persuasion. But "it would be irrational to look upon the isolation of neuropaths as a therapeutic necessity from which one might never depart. It only applies to particular cases." In proceeding to define the class of civilian patients for whom such methods are appropriate they emphasise the value of isolation for those whose troubles are due to, or aggravated by, "a bad family environment." In most cases the circumstances of the war-stricken soldier do not come within the categories which they suggest as justifying isolation. Moreover, most of the benefits which they attribute to this therapeutic measure, *i.e.*, removal from home surroundings and from the particular worries and anxieties which have caused the mischief, are attained (as we have already pointed out) when the soldier is an inmate of a special— or, in fact, of any—hospital.

When Déjerine and Gauckler proceed to define the different degrees in which the method of isolation may be practised; *viz.:* (1) strict isolation; (2) absolute isolation from one's family circle and environment, and (3) isolation from one's family circle alone, or from one's usual environment alone—it becomes clear that the treatment of every soldier who enters any hospital inevitably comes within the scope of categories 2 and 3.

Even when writing of hysterical women these French physicians tell us that—

"to show how slightly (their) experience has inclined (them) towards any systematic treatment of the psychoneuroses by isolation," isolation has not seemed (to the doctors) to be necessary for "at least a third of the neuropathic women who have been cared for at the Salpêtrière. Again, it must be added that, of the patients admitted, a certain number have been received at the hospital and naturally submitted to the dis-

cipline which belongs to an isolation ward much more for
humanitarian and social reasons than because absolute isolation seemed to be formally indicated." [1]

From the completely different nature of the circumstances of the nerve-stricken soldier and civilian respec-
tively it is clear that such total isolation can be considered
necessary for soldiers only in very few cases, even though
the modified forms of isolation, to which reference has
been made, may be useful for most of such patients.
The important point that emerges from this discussion
is the necessity which is laid upon the physician of determining, in the case of each individual patient, whether
isolation of any kind is desirable, what form it should
take, and especially when it should be used, modified or
discontinued.

*Suggestion and Hypnosis.* We have already touched
briefly on the need for sympathetic firmness and
for inspiring the patient with confidence that he will
recover. But such firmness can be useful only when
it is supported by respect for and confidence in the
physician. In most cases such respect can be gained
only by acquiring a real insight into the patient's condition and by treating him tactfully and reasonably. It
is too often forgotten that the neurasthenic patient's
continual and intense criticism of himself makes him
especially quick at intuitively becoming conscious of the
physician's failings. Under such circumstances, if the
doctor does not secure the patient's respect and convince
him that he really understands his condition, the former's
firmness and confident assurances will avail him nothing:
he has shown his hand; his failure will excite contempt;
and the patient's intractable, *enlightened* stubbornness

---

[1]*Op. cit.*, p. 315.

will be fatal to any further hope of influence on the part
of that particular physician.

Ever since mankind first sought help from his fellows for
his afflictions of body or mind, confidence in the efficiency
of the adviser's ability has been an essential factor in
leech-craft. To be able to convince a patient that he is
going to recover and that medical advice will help
towards that end is certainly not the least of the
physician's qualifications. But unless the assurances given
him are based upon real insight and understanding,
the process of securing the patient's confidence is not
very different from the charlatan's blatant boasting. In
other words, it is analogous to the confidence trick.

The confidence which is inspired in the patient by
his conviction of the physician's real understanding of
his condition is an altogether different matter. Such
" suggestion " necessarily enters into all successful treatment and this applies in a very special manner to the
cure of mental ailments.

But the question arises, is it useful or desirable to
supplement these measures of suggestion which are inci-
dental to all human intercourse, by more positive measures
of induced " suggestion " or hypnotism? There are wide
discrepancies of opinion with regard to this matter.
And, in endeavouring to come to a conclusion concerning it, it is important to eliminate as far as possible the
emotional tone which the warm discussion of this question
has aroused in the past.

The positive usefulness of hypnosis in relieving many
of the acute symptoms in recent cases of shell-shock has
been fully demonstrated by the important series of articles
by C. S. Myers, in the *Lancet*.[1] When it is possible by
such means to restore to the patient his lost memory or

---

[1] Feb. 13th, 1915 (p. 316); Jan. 8th, 1916 (p. 65); Mar.
18th, 1916 (p. 608); and Sept. 9th, 1916 p. 461).

speech or banish his despondency it often proves that the only hindrance to the complete restoration of his normal personality has been removed.

" It may be argued," to quote Myers's own account, " that mutism, rhythmical spasms, anæsthesiæ, and similar purely functional disturbances disappear after a time without specific treatment. But no one who has witnessed the unfeigned delight with which these patients, on waking from hypnosis, hail their recovery from such disorders can have any hesitation as to the impetus thus given towards a final cure. More especially is this the case in regard to the restoration of lost memories. Enough has already been said here about the striking changes in temperament, thought, and behaviour which follow on recovery from the amnesia. . . . The restoration to the normal self of the memories of scenes at one time dominant, now inhibited, and later tending to find occasional relief in abnormal states of consciousness or in disguised modes of expression—such restoration of past emotional scenes constitutes a first step towards obtaining that volitional control over them which the individual must finally acquire if he is to be healed.

Thus the minimal value that can be claimed for hypnosis in the treatment of shock cases consists in the preparation and facilitation of the path towards a complete recovery."[1]

Even if we admit that other measures, such as the administration of chloroform for the cure of hysterical mutism, may in some cases effect similar improvements, this should not blind us to the incontrovertible fact that hypnotism has been proved to be a valuable therapeutic agent in the early stages of shell-shock.

As a cure for certain patients who have passed the acute stages of shell-shock or other forms of war-strain, its use requires great discrimination in the selection of suitable cases and extreme care in its practice. It is very probable, too, that hypnotic suggestion by itself should never be regarded as sufficient treatment

[1] *Op. cit.*, p. 69.

for these cases, though undoubtedly it may be of great use as a part of such treatment.

A view endorsed by some well-known physicians is that all psychotherapy should be addréssed to the functions of consciousness, and that hypnosis, which is addressed to the functions of automatism, is therefore undesirable. As a general statement this is undoubtedly true of a great number of cases, but there occur instances in which it seems that this sensible rule may be wisely and judiciously broken. In some cases hypnosis helps in more quickly breaking down resistances, which occur in patients too beset by their own auto-suggestion and false beliefs to be able easily to grasp the arguments and persuasions which the physician may have spent days and weeks in vainly endeavouring to get accepted. Thus assistance may be sought without in any way interfering with subsequent treatment of the patient by psychological analysis and re-education.

The following instance illustrates the use of hypnotic suggestion in the manner described above.

The case was one of violent spasmodic tremor in the right arm of a soldier. When in a state of convalescence from a wound and shell-shock he suddenly encountered his company officer, to whom he was greatly attached. This officer had lost his right arm since he was last seen in France by the patient. The shock of suddenly meeting the officer in this condition set up the man's tremor. The case came under psychotherapeutic treatment some weeks later, when the patient, who was an extremely emotional individual, had lost all hope of recovery. Any attempt at purposive movements of the right hand and arm threw all the muscles of the right side of the body into a violent state of jerky tremor.

Long continued treatment by persuasion failed to effect any improvement whatsoever. The medical officer in charge of the case therefore decided to try hypnotic suggestion. This was easily carried out; the hypnotic state being moderately deep, though the patient was still in touch with his environment. Hope, courage and assurance of recovery *following his own effort*, together with determination to make every endeavour, were suggested to him. The patient was assured at each sitting that his nerves and muscles would every day respond more and more to his efforts at self-control. After a very few short sittings the man's hopeless attitude became changed to one of hope, effort and attention in the waking stage, and there was a slight but decided improvement in his voluntary power. Hypnotic suggestion was then given up, and the treatment was continued by means of encouragement, exercises and explanation of his trouble, with the result that two months later he was fit for discharge from the hospital.

It may reasonably be doubted whether methods of persuasion alone would have cured this man. In any case, it is clear that it would have taken a very long time. It is also probable that hypnotic suggestion alone, if continued, would very quickly have removed the symptoms. It may be doubted, however, whether it would have effected a permanent cure in a person so open to auto-suggestion. It seems, therefore, that a judicious combination of methods was advisable.

We are of the opinion that hypnotic treatment, when used with skill, discretion, and discrimination, has its place in the treatment of shell-shock and similar conditions, both in the acute and chronic stages.

In the majority of cases of some considerable duration, however, and in practically all those in which the trouble is due to some ante-war worry or emotion, it may be regarded as probable that hypnosis *alone* will be of relatively slight use and in many cases may be positively harmful, for under such circumstances, even with the most favourable conditions, it would result merely in

the removal of symptoms; and the removal of one
may be followed by the appearance of another, which
may even be induced by the process of hypnosis. Moreover, in cases where there is a tendency to the development of a double personality hypnosis may have the
effect of increasing the risk. Further, if the patient
has sufficient of his own will-power to enable the process
of re-education to be carried out, it is clearly undesirable,
both on psychological and ethical grounds, for the doctor
to impress his influence from without.

In considering the possibility of the usefulness of
hypnotic suggestion it is important to bear in mind that
various factors may come into play in impressing an
event upon the patient's memory, or in determining the
effect of the shock from which he is suffering when he
arrives in hospital. In the first place there is the
vividness or intensity of the stimulus; in the second,
the degree of recency; in the third, the frequency of the
stimulus; and in the fourth its relevancy. By the latter
is meant the extent to which a given event appeals to
the individual's past experience, and becomes integrated
into his personality.

A patient who has recently received a severe shock,
the effects of which alone represent the real trouble,
without the disturbance of any antecedent experience,
might quite well be relieved by hypnotic suggestion from
sleeplessness, pain, or amnesia; and in some cases this
removal of the acute symptoms which determine the
persistence of the shock effects may lead to complete
recovery. A single and sudden wholly irrelevant experience, such as the bursting of a shell, which has no
relationship whatever to the patient's past experience,
and produces effects by its vividness and its recency,
might quite well be neutralised by another kind of wholly
irrelevant intrusion, such as hypnotic suggestion. This
argument may perhaps be made more intelligible by a

homely analogy. A temperate man walking along the
street might be thrown temporarily into a condition of
faintness or collapse by seeing some ghastly accident,
but by taking a "brandy and soda," which to such a
man would be a wholly irrelevant experience, the
physiological expressions of his emotions might be con-
trolled and he might be able to proceed on his way, and
to overcome completely the effects of the transitory
occurrence. But in the case of a man who, for example,
had been greatly worried by monetary troubles for a
number of years, the "brandy and soda" would not
produce anything more than a temporary alleviation of
his troubles. The latter illustration represents the
chronic psychosis which, as Déjerine has so admirably
explained, is quite unsuitable for hypnotic treatment.
But the distinguished French neurologist's statements do
not seem to apply to the former type of case, due to a
vivid recent shock, in the symptomatology of which
troubles before the shock play no part. In such cases
the results of hypnotic suggestion are often brilliant, if
erratic, as is the "brandy and soda cure" for the man
who is overcome by a sudden terrible experience in the
street.

There are, however, patients who have not sufficient
will-power or intelligence to be properly re-educated, to
whom a certain amount of suggestion may be of some
use.

Those who have used hypnosis in civil practice are
aware that in certain individual cases of long-standing
trouble, such, for example, as chronic alcoholism, hypnotic treatment is of unquestionable value. Among
soldiers suffering from the long-standing effects of shell-
shock, hypnosis may be able in some cases to help in
the restoration of health with an effectiveness that no
other method can rival.

Both the danger and the possible usefulness of hyp-

notism may be illustrated by an actual case. It is that of
a man all of whose companions were destroyed by the
bursting of a shell, and who suffered for months afterwards
from complete loss of memory. A medical man hypnotised
him, and perhaps with undue tactlessness, brought back
the memory of the critical incident at the front, stripped
of all the episodes which led up to or followed it.
This excited in him the most violent emotions, and
he became sick with terror; for the revived incident seemed
perfectly real to him, or, as he described it afterwards, " it
jumped up against him," and for weeks he was so utterly
terrified that he would not go near the doctor. Even
though he could not retain the memory of any other
recent events the horror of that experience seemed to
have made him remember his dread of a particular
medical man. But by making use of the information
gained during that revival under hypnosis of an incident
unknown to anyone but the patient, which his amnesia
up till then had kept sealed up, it became possible for
another medical officer to bridge the gap between his
memory of previous events and the experiences which
the patient was known to have had in the military
hospitals.

In speaking of the results of hypnotic treatment as
being brilliant but erratic, it is important to remember
that the same observations apply to suggestion without
hypnosis. For instance, the application of electricity to
the vocal cords in cases of hysterical aphonia affords
an admirable illustration of the treatment by suggestion,
even if the method savours of charlatanism. An excellent
demonstration of the part which psychical factors play in
such cases is afforded by the story of a sailor on the
German battle-cruiser *Derfflinger*, recorded by Blässig.[1]

---

[1]*Münchener Medizinische Wochenschrift*, June 15th, 1915,
p. 335.

" A seaman from the *Derfflinger* was brought into a naval hospital with loss of voice on Dec. 22nd, 1914, and could speak only in a whisper. He said that he had always had good health, with the exception that as a child he had diphtheria, but recovered without tracheotomy or any complication. His voice had always been clear and well under control. At the beginning of December he had a slight cold, which he attributed to sentry duty on deck in very stormy and wet weather. While in the ammunition chamber of the big guns he was greatly upset during the firing and suddenly lost his voice. After fourteen days he recovered his speech. On Feb. 12th, 1915, he returned to hospital with complete loss of voice, immediately after the naval engagement in the North Sea. On Feb. 15th he was treated with electricity, directly applied to the vocal cords, and on March 20th he was discharged with complete recovery of his speech. But on returning to duty, as soon as he went on board his ship his voice was suddenly lost for the third time, and he remained aphonic."

This is clear evidence of the fact that his trauma was psychical. His previous history perhaps contains the clue explaining why, in his case, it was his voice which was affected. The application of the faradic current was suggestion pure and simple.

In emphasising the limited usefulness and possible danger of suggestive therapeutics in many cases that are not quite recent, we have not been referring to that method of suggestion which is involved to a greater or less degree in all successful treatment of disease—the process of gaining the patient's confidence and impressing him with the idea that he is going to recover.

" The conversational attitude, the familiar manner of talking things over, the heart-to-heart discussion, where the physician must exert his good sense and feeling, and the patient be willing to be confidential " is the method which Déjerine calls ' psychotherapy by *persuasion*.' " It consists in explaining to the patient the true reasons for his condition, and [for] the different functional manifestations which he presents, and above all, in establishing the patient's confidence in himself and awakening the different elements of his personality, so as to make them capable of becoming the starting-point of the effort which will enable him to regain his self-control. The exact comprehension of the phenomena which he presents must be gained by the patient by means of his own reasoning. . . . The part that the physician plays is simply to recall, awaken, and direct . . . "[1]

No one who has not had the experience of guiding mental patients in the way so lucidly expounded by the French physicians can form any adequate conception of the remarkable efficacy of these common-sense methods in restoring to those who are afflicted a normal attitude of mind. It is certainly saving considerable numbers of soldiers from the fate of insanity. These methods are not novel, even if the fuller comprehension of their mode of operation is only dawning upon us now. This point has been admirably expounded by Déjerine and Gauckler, from whose book we must quote once more:—

" May we be permitted to quote a few lines in which Bernardin de St. Pierre has defined, more exactly and better perhaps than we could do, and with a sort of prescience of what is needed, the very rôle that we would like to [see our physicians adopt towards their patients].

I wish that there might be formed in large cities an establishment, somewhat resembling those which charitable physicians and wise jurists have formed in Paris, to remedy the evils both of the body and of one's fortunes; I mean councils for consolation, where an unfortunate, sure of his secret being kept and even of his incognito, might bring up the subject of his troubles. We have, it is true, confessors and preachers to whom the sublime function of offering consolation to the unfortunate seems to be reserved. But the confessors are not always at the disposition of their penitents. As for the preachers, their sermons serve more as nourishment for souls than as a remedy, for they do not preach against boredom, or unhappiness, or scruples, or melancholy, or vexation, or ever so many other evils which affect the soul. It is not easy to find in a timid and depressed personality the exact point about which he is grieving, and to pour balm into his wounds

[1] Déjerine and Gauckler, *op. cit.*, p. 283.

with the hand of the Samaritan. It is an art known only to sensitive and sympathetic souls.

Oh! if only men who knew the science of grief could give unfortunate people the benefit of their experience and sympathy, many miserable souls would come to seek from them the consolation which they cannot get from preachers or all the books of philosophy in the world. Often, to comfort the troubles of men, all that is necessary is to find out from what they are suffering (*Etude de la Nature*, 1784)."

Déjerine and Gauckler add:—

"One could not express any better, or any more directly, what we never cease to maintain, however lacking in science it may seem at the first—namely, the real therapeutic action of kindness.

Liberated morally, and having regained consciousness of self, and freed in addition from his functional manifestations by the appropriate processes . . . the patient is cured. He is cured from his actual attack. But his mental foundation, his psychological constitution, still remains in the same condition which permitted him under emotional influences to become a neurasthenic. The rôle of the physician is, therefore, not ended. He must still build up his patient's life, still practise prophylaxis, and get the patient into a condition where his character will be established.[1]

*Rational Treatment.* So far in this chapter we have been discussing what may be described as general methods of treatment, which do not *necessarily* involve any attempt to probe into distinctive individual symptoms and to discover the real fundamental cause or causes of the trouble. The measures so far considered are empirical rather than rational. But they are the only methods of treatment discussed in most of the text-books. It is an axiom in medicine that correct diagnosis is the indispensable preliminary to the rational and intelligent treatment of disease. This fundamental principle is universally recognised in dealing with bodily affections;

---

[1]*Op. cit.*, pp. 302-3.

but it is the primary object of this book to insist that
*it is equally necessary to observe the same principle in
the case of mental illness.*

It may seem ironical to stress this elementary consideration, but it is notorious that accurate diagnosis is
too often ignored in cases of incipient mental disturbance.
It is idle to pretend that such a procedure is unnecessary,
or to urge in extenuation of the failure to search for
causes that many patients recover under the influence of
nothing more than rest, quiet, and ample diet.

Many mild cases of illness, whether bodily or mental,
may and do recover even if undiagnosed or untreated.
But on the other hand many mild cases get worse; and
it is the primary duty of the physician correctly to
diagnose the nature of the trouble and to give a prog-
nosis—to decide whether the illness is mild or severe.
Some of the most serious cases of incipient mental
trouble are those of patients who do not seem to be
really ill, and are easily overlooked by a visiting physician.
They are quiet and inoffensive and display no obvious
signs of the insidious processes that are at work in them.
But all the time they may be, and often are, brooding
over some grievance or moral conflict, worrying about
their feelings, misinterpreting them and gradually
systematising these misunderstandings until they become
set as definite delusions or hallucinations. If, acting on
the belief that it is bad to talk about a patient's worries,
the physician leaves such a man alone, he is clearly
neglecting his obvious duty. For the whole trouble may
be due to some trivial misunderstanding which he could
easily correct.

In the severer forms of mental disease, precise diagnosis
is even more intimately related to treatment than in the
case of bodily illness. For when a patient's illness is
recognised as some bodily affliction, such as pneumonia
or appendicitis, certain general lines of treatment are laid

down as soon as the appropriate label has been found
for the complaint, though, in the case of the latter
illness, there is added the further problem of whether or
not surgical interference is indicated.

In cases of mental disturbance, however, the general
lines of treatment cannot thus arbitrarily be determined
merely by finding an appropriate label. It is true that
as in the treatment of bodily disease, certain general
principles must be observed, such as the provision of
abundant and suitable food, and the protection of the
patient from all disturbing influences. But the essence
of the mentally afflicted patient's trouble is some particular form of anxiety or worry which is *individual and
personal.* The aim of the diagnosis, therefore, should
be not merely to determine the appropriate generic
label for the affliction, but rather to discover the particular circumstances which have given rise to the present
state. The special object of the physician should be to
remove or nullify the exciting cause of the disturbance;
and in order to do this it is essential that he should
discover the precise nature of the trouble. The diagnosis,
therefore, must be of a different nature from that
demanded in case of physical illness, where the condition
may be adequately defined by some such generic term
as "lobar pneumonia" or "acute appendicitis," and its
gravity estimated by the general condition and physique
of the patient. In the case of mental trouble, the
physician has to make an individual diagnosis, based not
only upon an insight into the personality but also into
the particular anxieties of each patient.

But even when it is recognised that exact diagnosis of
the particular circumstances of each individual patient is
essential, if the trouble is to be treated rationally and
with insight, there still remain many difficult problems
as to procedure.

Amongst those whom experience has convinced of the

efficacy of psychological treatment for this class of case, there are indications of a divergence of opinion in the matter of procedure. Some believe that it is sufficient if the medical man has discovered the real cause of the trouble and explained it to the patient. Other workers look upon a preliminary psychical examination merely as a means of diagnosis, the unveiling of the hidden cause of the trouble; and consider that the treatment should be the laborious and often lengthy process of re-educating the patient, and so restoring to him the proper control of himself. It is of the utmost importance to emphasise the undoubted fact that those who maintain either of these views to the exclusion of the other are committing a grievous and dangerous error, for there is no sharp line of demarcation between the two procedures.

A sensible and intelligent man, once the cause of his trouble has been made clear to him, may be competent to continue to cure himself, or, in other words, to re-educate himself, and completely to conquer the cause of his undoing. But the duller and stupider man may need a daily demonstration and renewal of confidence before he begins to make any progress. It is precisely analogous to the experience of every teacher of a class of students; the brilliant man will seize hold of a principle at once and learn to apply it without further help, whereas the dull man needs repeated and concrete demonstrations before it sinks into his understanding.

In dealing with soldiers, and this applies with especial force to the regular army, the conditions in many of the cases differ considerably from those of the civilians. Trifling forgetfulness in the civilian would perhaps not be a serious cause of worry, but in the soldier, inured by years of training to strict discipline, forgetfulness of even trivial instructions, or any difficulty in understanding complex orders, is likely to bring down upon his head condign punishment. Such lapses are regarded by the soldier as extremely serious offences, because years of training and discipline have inculcated this idea. When as the result of shock such soldiers are afflicted by even slight forgetfulness, they become worried by it much more than would the civilian and exaggerate its importance until it becomes a real terror to them. As the result of their training they may regard such phenomena as altogether abnormal; and by a process of rationalising what to them is a novel experience, they are apt to imagine that they are going mad. Such patients often dream about incidents in their army life when they had been forgetful and got into trouble; they become obsessed with the haunting fear that they are likely to get into perpetual difficulties, are worried by the thought that they are incompetent for the duties to which they have been accustomed, and may imagine themselves debarred from all useful work. However, they are easily reassured when the medical attendant explains to them that in ordinary life civilians are frequently subject to such experiences, and that it is only the special circumstances of army life which make such trivial lapses seem serious to them. Not only is the soldier much more scared by such things than the civilian, but it is also a very remarkable phenomenon, and certainly one which came as a surprise, that the neurasthenia of a soldier is apt to be very much more serious than that of the civilian. For when a really brave man is stricken by fear he is more seriously affected by the terror of an experience which to him not only has a larger element of novelty than in the case of the civilian, but also wounds him more deeply by convincing him that he is lacking in that very quality which is most essential for his professional work.

### The Therapeutic Value of Work.

It should be unnecessary to emphasise the desirability of preventing the neurasthenic from dwelling upon his subjective troubles by occupying his mind with other things. This end may often be achieved by the provision of suitable occupation, and where possible, for many obvious reasons, this occupation should take the form of useful work. The worker then feels that he is not a mere burden upon the hospital which is treating him: the institution in its turn benefits materially. But it is necessary to sound a note of warning against the indiscriminate prescription of work as a panacea. First of all it should be certain that the work is of such a kind as really to interest the patient and to occupy his mind. There are many varieties of work, especially of manual labour, which can be performed mechanically, and do not succeed in distracting the attention from worries and anxieties. But more important even than this is the consideration that there are some mental troubles from which no form of work will distract the patient. Especially is this the case in many of the psychoneuroses caused by the war. The sufferer is often haunted day and night by memories which torture him not merely by their horror but also by another aspect which is even worse: the ever-increasing moral remorse which they induce. A patient may be troubled not only by the terrible nature of the memory but by the recurring thought, " If I had not done this or that, " it might never have happened." The reader will easily see how such a thought may arise in the mind, especially of a nerve-stricken officer or " N.C.O." after weeks of brooding in private upon the memory of a disaster. Now, such self-reproaches are frequently based upon entirely insufficient evidence, and if the medical officer is given the opportunity of calmly discussing their foundations with the patient, the result is often to reassure him and to enable him to view his past in an entirely new light. It is then, and not before then, that he will be able cheerfully to enter upon useful occupation and to benefit by it. To suppose that the mere physical fatigue induced by a day's hard work will banish all forms of insomnia betrays an ignorance of one of the most important causes of this malady; *viz.*, mental conflict. It is well known that bodily fatigue in the case of a mentally excited patient may merely increase his unrest at night. Again, anyone who has had a few months' experience of receiving the confidence of these nerve-stricken soldiers will know that some of their troubles are so poignant that the attractions of the (apparently) most interesting kinds of occupation leave them cold.

To sum up, the physician may confidently prescribe work when, by investigating the history of any particular case, he has satisfied himself that such occupation will be likely successfully and profitably to distract the patient's mind from his worries. But the prescription of work for the patient must be regarded as a sequel to, not as a substitute for, the performance of work by the doctor.

# CHAPTER III.

# Psychological Analysis and Re-education.

THE methods of treatment which have been described in the foregoing pages: sympathy, firmness, isolation, suggestion in its various forms, and hypnosis; while all useful in their proper place, often prove to be of no avail in cases of psychoneurosis. Where the distressing symptoms lie on the surface so that both they and their causes are easily discoverable by the physician—if, indeed, they have not been known from the beginning, to the patient himself—it is sometimes possible to bring about a complete cure without any very penetrating analysis by the doctor of the mental antecedents of the patient's present condition. Thus, for example, a courageous and keen soldier who, suffering from loss of sleep and from the harassing experiences of the battlefield, eventually breaks down, the precipitating cause perhaps being shell-shock, may need little more to set him on his legs than the comfort, assiduous attention, and pleasant distractions of a Red Cross hospital. For the civilian whose chief trouble is the irritability caused by a multiplicity of minor business worries, or family jars, a few days of isolation, giving perhaps, among the other benefits which we have mentioned, the opportunity to think things out, may have excellent results. The beneficent action of hypnosis in removing the acute disturbances caused by shell-shock has already been illustrated. But a large number of cases fall into none of these categories. Sympathy merely annoys them, isolation tortures them, for besides letting them think—usually in a very unwise way—it helps to confirm their impression that they are seriously ill, just because it involves the treatment of them as special cases. Suggestive measures may be to them like water on a duck's back, and hypnosis may prove of no avail. Firmness may have merely the effect of proving to the doctor that there exist patients firmer than himself. But, fortunately, psychical methods are not exhausted. There still remains at least one—that of psychological analysis and re-education.

The employment of psychological analysis in medicine means the resolution of the patient's mental condition into its essential elements, just as by chemical analysis it is possible to determine that water, for example, is composed of certain definite proportions of oxygen and hydrogen combined in a particular way. Re-education is the helping of the patient, by means of the new knowledge gained by analysis, to face life's difficulties anew.

It is sometimes urged that if this be all that is meant by psychological analysis, alienists have been doing this ever since insanity was first treated, nay, further, doctors have been practising it since the time of Hippocrates. It is pointed out that when a patient is first interviewed by the physician, an inquiry is always made into his mental state and behaviour, and into the presence of delusions and hallucinations or other unusual mental phenomena. His relatives are questioned concerning the relation of his recent behaviour to that at the time when he was considered normal. Now the answer to this assertion is that such an investigation is useful, indispensable in fact, but it cannot be called psychological analysis.

The point may become clearer to the untechnical reader if he will imagine for a moment that a carver, skilled in separating the legs and wings from the body of a bird, should claim to be practising anatomy. The anatomist would at once object that while such separation of limbs from trunk is a small detail which sometimes forms part of the anatomist's task, it can scarcely be called more than a preliminary to his study. For first of all, while to a carver a leg is an ultimate unit, to the anatomist it is, for the naked eye, a collection of bones, muscles, tendons, skin, nerves, veins, arteries, nails and the rest, and, seen through the microscope, a tremendous organisation of infinitely more complex structures. Furthermore, it might be pointed out that merely to separate these more minute structures into their constituent parts and to name them, by no means constitutes the whole of the work of the intelligent anatomist. He wishes to study the inter-relations of these parts, the way in which they work together for the common good of the leg. And lastly, the leg must not be studied only in separation from the trunk, for its functions are subordinate to the requirements of the body as a whole.

So, in the same way, to record that a man is suffering from a delusion of persecution or an unreasonable fear of open spaces is merely to "carve up" the condition of his mind. First of all it must be ascertained how far that delusion has interpenetrated with the rest of his mental life; whether, for example, his false belief is restricted to a specific kind of persecution from a particular person, or is a general delusion that everybody and everything in the world is against him. And again, if the delusion is strictly specific, it is important to know whether it has been the cause of secondary false beliefs, produced by rationalisation, to buttress the primary delusion against the inevitable contradiction from facts which it would otherwise suffer.

Further, the nature of the delusion must be analysed. Why is it of this and not of that persecution? Why is this particular person feared or hated? Is it a constant factor in the patient's existence, or does it break out at certain times? If so, the patient's life at these critical periods must be carefully examined. The doctor must discover where the patient was at the time, what he was doing and thinking, who were his companions, and so on.

Next comes the important inquiry into the history of the delusion. And here, just as the anatomist is able nowadays to mobilise for service all his knowledge of comparative anatomy and evolution, so if the physician has really scientific knowledge, not only of the delusions in other patients, but also of the development of ordinary beliefs in sane people,[1] he will be immensely helped in his search, and may be enabled thereby to make many short cuts to the essential facts. He will endeavour to date the important stages of development of the delusion; to find a time when, so far as the patient knows, his mind was free from it.

Thus we may say that a psychological investigation of a case of mental disorder dissects its normal as well as its abnormal phenomena into their functional elements. Compared with the procedure which merely records such gross units as delusions or hallucinations, it is as anatomy to mere carving, however skilful the latter may be.

But the psychological investigation is not merely comparable to anatomical dissection. We have also compared the mind to a chemical compound, rather than a mechanical mixture. Especially is this true not only of the normal but also of the abnormal mind, when the latter has had time to settle down into its new

---

[1]Such development involves a complicated set of processes the nature of which is by no means obvious to unaided common sense.

position of relative equilibrium and integration; when, for example, a delusion has become so fixed that the patient's life is entirely ordered in obedience to it, and he has ceased to have any doubts as to its reality or to struggle against its domination.[1] It is only when the warring elements in the mind are relatively independent, and before they have succeeded in "making terms" with each other, that the mind even remotely resembles a mechanical mixture. It follows, therefore, that psychological analysis of a case of mental disorder is usually comparable to *chemical analysis* as well as to anatomical dissection.

Now the most striking result of chemical analysis is to show that the appearance and general properties of the elements composing a compound are different from the appearance and properties of the compound itself. This is exactly the case, too, with mental analysis. A mere dissection of an abnormal condition is sometimes sufficient in the milder cases to serve as the basis for curative measures,[2] but in more advanced cases, or those of longer standing, real analysis is necessary in order to get at the unknown factors.

It is just at this point that a number of investigators of mental disorder decline to go any farther on the path of research. Up to this stage, they say, one is relying upon ascertained facts, for one has the warrant of the patient's own memory for the data obtained. Further analysis of a mental phenomenon must inevitably involve appeal to unconscious factors. And, once one

---

[1] ". . . for example, a patient may maintain that he is the king, but that an organised conspiracy exists to deprive him of his birthright. In this way delusions are sometimes elaborated into an extraordinarily complicated system and every fact of the patient's experience is distorted until it is capable of taking its place in the delusional scheme." Bernard Hart, *The Psychology of Insanity*, Cambridge, 1914, p. 32.

[2] *Cf.* p. 15*f.*

has called in the unconscious as a means of explanation, psychology becomes a mere "tumbling ground for whimsies."

Probably there are few people to whom this statement does not appear to express the universal verdict of common sense. That is precisely what it does. But it should be unnecessary to point out that common sense alone is not always the most reliable guide to the discovery of fact. Unaided common sense not only informed men for centuries that the sun moved round the earth, but told them so with such finality and conviction that extraordinarily unpleasant consequences ensued for those who did not believe in such an obvious fact. And the old belief, wholly false as it is, has still to be unlearnt by every child.

In the same way, the 'common sense' point of view which we have described is not flawless. It assumes that a patient is able not only to surmount the great difficulties of translating his experiences and beliefs precisely into words—a difficult task even for the well-educated person—but also to account for and explain them truthfully.

It may, however, be pointed out that, though this last-mentioned misleading assumption is widespread, it is by no means so universal or so tenacious in man as the "belief of his own senses" that the sun goes round the earth. In fact, quite apart from the teachings of modern psychology, we frequently find well-founded suspicions in the lay mind that a man is not always competent to give the basis of and reasons for his mental condition. This view is summed up in the famous advice to the future judge, "Give your decision, it will probably be right. But do not give your reasons, they will almost certainly be wrong."[1]

---

[1] Cf. Hart, op. cit., p. 66.

What ordinary man, unversed in the subtleties of theology or comparative religion, could give to an agnostic a satisfactory account of the reason why—being let us say, a Christian, and a Protestant Christian—he is a Primitive Methodist or an English Presbyterian? Let us complicate the matter further by supposing that this sect to which he now belongs is not that in which he was brought up by his family! Many of the factors which have contributed to his present religious beliefs may have been entirely forgotten now, recallable only with the greatest difficulty[1] and with the help of a second person skilful in such investigation.

We may take as a good example of the historical complexity of significant attitudes and actions in life, the process of falling in love—especially if it is not, or at least seems not to be, love at first sight. It is generally admitted that, in the development of this psychological phenomenon, onlookers see most of the game. In other words, the actions of the two persons who are gradually becoming more and more attracted to each other are partly determined by motives, which, unknown to them, are patent to their observant relations and friends.

Further examples may be given to illustrate this important and oft-disputed point. Let us suppose that a musical critic, after hearing a new symphony by an unconventional composer, immediately writes a lengthy appreciation of the performance. It is clear that nobody would expect him to be able to give, off-hand, an account of his reasons for every sentence of the criticism. But it is obvious

---

[1] The reader may pass an interesting time in trying to give himself or others an historical account of the events in his life which caused him to choose his present profession. He will probably find that memories emerge of incidents and conversations which have been forgotten for years. Yet he may find that they have influenced his present life and his action at any moment of the present, to a very great extent. Their present action clearly has been unconscious.

that a single phrase in this account may be but the apex of a whole pyramid of memories emanating from the critic's technical training, his attitude towards the new departure, experiences highly coloured with emotion which a few notes of the music may have evoked, and his mental condition at the time he heard the performance. Nobody denies that these may have shaped or even determined his criticism. But who believes either that they were all conscious at the time of writing the article, or that he could resuscitate them without much time and trouble and perhaps the help of a cross-examiner?

Again, there are occasions when society expects that a man shall be unconscious of the reasons for some of his actions. He is expected, for example, to behave politely, attentively and chivalrously to ladies, not because at the moment of taking the outside of the pavement he remembers why he does so, but simply because he has been brought up in this way. And conversely, too conscious politeness in a man arouses in others—and often rightly—the suspicion that it is a recent acquisition.

We see then that it is rare for a man to be able to give a true account, even to himself, of the reasons underlying his important acts and beliefs, when his mental condition is relatively calm and his social relationships are normal. But when a case of mental disorder is in question it becomes quite obvious that the patient is frequently not in a position to give, either to himself or to another, anything like a complete or true enumeration and description of the antecedent experiences which have brought about his present condition.

It therefore becomes necessary to admit that unconscious factors of great importance may play an influential part in the production of mental disorder and that, therefore, some way must be found of tapping these submerged streams.

The most direct way into the complexities of the unconscious mental processes of a person is afforded by a study of his more "unusual" actions and thoughts. For few persons are so completely adapted to their environment or so perfectly balanced that moments never arise in which their mental behaviour is not surprising, either to themselves or to others. And even the Admirable Crichtons of our acquaintance are not entirely immune from errant moments—at least in their sleep. The dream, then, is the chief gate by which we can enter into the knowledge of the unconscious. For in sleep, the relatively considerable control which most of us in waking life possess over the coming and going of mental events is almost if not entirely abrogated. Thoughts and desires, which, if they attempted to dominate consciousness in waking life, would be promptly suppressed, arise, develop and expand to an astounding extent in the dream.

This statement, of course, is entirely independent of the implications of any one "theory of dreams." Its truth is evident to anyone who has honestly recorded or considered his own dreams for even a short period.

Other unusual mental processes are manifested in such events as "slips of the tongue," "slips of the pen," the mislaying of important objects, the forgetting of significant facts, or conversely the inability to get an apparently unimportant memory out of one's mind. All these phenomena, common enough in the normal individual, are usually more frequent in the abnormal mind. Besides the patient's voluntary account of, and comments upon, these events,[1] other methods of obtaining data are possible to

[1]It should not be forgotten that when a patient in an early stage of mental disorder voluntarily seeks the doctor, his *active co-operation* in the task of tracing the causal factors of his trouble is of the greatest value. This assistance cannot be relied upon after the patient has been certified as insane and removed to an asylum, or even after he has been taken to the

the physician. He will note the matters about which in conversation the patient is apt to become silent, embarrassed or inexplicably irritated, to hesitate, to say he has forgotten, or even to lie. All these sidelights upon the mental make-up are carefully noted by the physician and the deductions from them compared, not only with the patient's accounts of himself on different days—narratives which when put together may show important discrepancies and thin places—but also with the information obtainable from his family. These devices serve to bring to light in an extraordinary manner a whole number of memories, many of them of immense significance for the comprehension of the patient's present mental state, which it would be utterly impossible to discover in mere conversation or even by cross-questioning.

It is sometimes felt that these methods which savour strongly of catching the patient tripping, while they may unearth some interesting details of his past life, do no more than exhibit under a strong magnifying glass a few minute excrescences upon his otherwise fair mental countenance. But it should be pointed out that nobody who has ever honestly collected together and compared the memories which have coalesced to compose a dozen of his dreams—especially if he has done so with the help and under the cross-examination of a candid friend who

---

doctor at the instance of others. For obvious reasons he is then more likely to hide than to reveal his eccentricities. The simulation of insanity is comparatively rare: it is difficult and usually easily detected. It is dissimulation—the concealment of symptoms of disease—which is the doctor's greatest enemy. The deluded man may hide his delusions because "everyone knows that these beliefs are mad:" the melancholic may pretend for the time to be cheerful in order that his liberty may not be interfered with. (*Cf*. K. Jasper's *Allgemeine Psychopathologie*, Berlin, 1913, p. 317.) Such attitudes of the patient are obviously strengthened by our present custom of delaying the treatment of mental disorder.

knows him well—will maintain that the material thus found is unimportant. As Professor Freud says, "The dream never occupies itself with trifles." It is probably just because the thoughts and desires underlying the dreams have been refused their normal outlet, that they express themselves in such bizarre forms.

Moreover, the fact should not be overlooked that in other sciences—including the most exact, the physical sciences—the most profoundly important general conclusions are often arrived at by the examination of unusual phenomena, of nature "caught tripping." The study of the thunderstorm was the foundation of our present knowledge of that great force which is active not only in thunderstorms but throughout all matter. Observation of the sporadic and relatively unusual volcanic eruptions of the mind may prove to be an important foundation of our future knowledge of general psychology. As in the inorganic, so in the organic world, there is no sharp line dividing normal from abnormal, and the unusual phenomenon is sometimes simpler and more easily studied than the usual, as "Sherlock Holmes" was so fond of demonstrating.[1] From a scientific standpoint, then, we have every justification for pressing to the utmost our study of the unusual mental phenomena exhibited by the patient, and for our belief that their nature is not unimportant, but highly significant for therapeutical purposes.

.Another objection, however, is frequently levelled

---

[1]In his account of the wonderful exploits of "Sherlock Holmes," Sir Arthur Conan Doyle was merely applying, with inimitable skill and literary resourcefulness, the methods of clinical diagnosis in medicine to the detection of imaginary crimes. The unusual phenomenon in medicine or in crime often affords the most obvious clue to the expert who can appreciate its significance, whereas a simple dyspepsia or a common-place murder may present insoluble problems, because they reveal no distinctive signs to guide the investigator.

against such a procedure, from quite a different direction,
or rather from a number of directions.   This objection
can be expressed simply in words, such as "One ought not
to probe so deeply into a patient's innermost mental life,"
and is not to be met by a single argument.   The reason is
that it is polyhedral in form, and that each of its faces
or aspects must be considered separately.   For it should
be obvious to everyone that such an objection cannot
be flippantly waved away.

The aspects of this question which seem to have more
particularly appealed to the critics of the method which
we are describing, are at least four in number, which
we may describe as the æsthetic, social, medical and
moral.

The origin of the first, the æsthetic aspect, is easily
seen.   It is quite clear that in the investigation of the
inmost secrets of a person's life (and particularly of a
life which has become so entangled and complicated that
the help of another is sought for its restoration to 'mental
tidiness ') there must emerge frequently much that the
patient finds unpleasant to relate.   When we remember
that a neurosis often (perhaps always) occurs as a result
of the patient's inability to adjust his instinctive demands
to the opportunities of his environment, it becomes clear
that in the investigation of his history discussion is
inevitable of mental events in which the fundamental
instincts have played a great part.   Now, of those important instinctive impulses, it is obvious that in a civilised
community few are so often thwarted, deliberately re-
pressed, or otherwise obstructed as the powerful one of
sex.   It therefore follows that in a large number of cases
the discussion of sexual matters becomes unavoidable.
Some critics have seized on this point as the weak spot
against which to launch their attacks, descanting upon the
unpleasantness, even the nauseousness, of such discussion.
Not all of them, however, make it clear whether in their

opinion it is the patient or the doctor who should be shielded from such unpleasant experiences. If the latter, the verdict of society would probably be that the sooner a man requiring such protection was excused not only from these uncongenial duties, but from all medical obligations whatever, the better for the community. If the former, it may be pointed out that every reasonable person will agree that the man who does not tell the whole truth to his doctor or his lawyer is a fool. Furthermore, even under present conditions, if it be considered advisable in the interests of the patient's bodily health, the doctor does not hesitate to ask, and the patient to answer, questions about the most intimate matters, some of them literally and not merely metaphorically nauseous.

We may therefore dismiss the æsthetic objection as unworthy of the consideration either of a conscientious doctor, or of a reasonable patient.

We may turn now to what we have designated the social aspect of the objection. It should need little explanation. There has arisen a convention, subscribed to consciously or unconsciously by many, that the doctor shall ask and the patient answer quite freely questions relating to the patient's bodily well-being, but that any unusual mental occurrences must be considered the patient's private affair into which it is not the business of the doctor to pry.

It would be rash to deny that up to a certain point this convention is susceptible of defence. But, carried too far, it is productive of disastrous results. Moreover, it is impossible for a doctor to treat many varieties even of physical disease without becoming to a great extent the confidant not only of the patient but often of his family. And there is no doubt that the present unwritten law that the doctor should confine himself to the patient's physical ills is often judiciously disobeyed by very many successful practitioners. Yet it must be recognised that the convention exists, and like all social usages is extremely tenacious.

The chief medical objection, which we shall now consider, is usually expressed in some such form as the assertion that "it makes the patient worse to talk about his worries" and that one should rather "try to make him forget them." Let us examine these statements, both of which contain a certain amount of truth, but if applied without qualification to serious cases of incipient mental disorder can by their respective negative and positive tendencies do an incalculable amount of harm. They are often the result of applying experience acquired by the successful reassuring of a certain type of "malade imaginaire," to the consideration of far more complicated cases in which such easy and straightforward treatment is impossible. A man, let us say, visits a doctor and confesses to him his fear that he is suffering from some organic disease. The physician after a careful examination proves to the patient by objective means that there is nothing the matter with him; the sufferer is reassured and returns to his daily business and in due course forgets about this worry or ceases to be troubled by the memory of it. Here the diagnosis, treatment, and cure may be uncomplicated and "on the surface." But even here it should be emphasised that in one sense, far from "making the patient worse" to talk about his trouble, the talking about it was the *sine quâ non* of cure; otherwise the doctor would never have known of the fear. In another sense, however, talking about the trouble did make the sufferer worse—but for a short time only, during a confession of his apprehensions, or perhaps even for a few days, if more than one visit to the consulting room were necessary before the doctor's verdict could be obtained.

But not all visits to the doctor end so briefly or so easily as this. The patient's trouble, on examination, may

prove to be organic and of long standing. Does the
doctor consider then that it is his duty to emulate the
Christian Scientist or to "make the patient forget it?"
On the contrary, he does not flinch from the employment
of the most searching methods of investigation, lengthy
and often painful treatment, and, if it seems necessary
in the patient's interest, he will carry out or arrange for
operative interference which may be difficult, expensive,
by no means free from danger, and is quite likely to
"make the patient worse," perhaps for a considerable
time, before its beneficial results appear.

It is therefore idle to argue that on the one hand
psychological methods of treating mental disorder are
unnecessary because some patients get better without
their application; while, on the other, they are dangerous
because they may make a patient worse. The same remarks
could be applied to most of the successful operative
methods of present-day medicine. All of them are fraught
with grave potentiality for harm if applied by unskilled
persons.

The degree to which the doctor is medically justified
in probing the patient's intimacies is obviously dependent
upon the individual case. Not all patients require such
drastic incisions; a fact which has been clearly shown in
the special military hospitals. An intelligent man of
strong will, whose social relations have hitherto been
normal and happy, might be temporarily "bowled over"
by the emotional stress of the campaign, but after a few
inquiries into the causes of his mental anguish and a few
explanations, he is often set on his feet again.

We must not forget, however, the other side of the
picture. There are many patients, who, far from being
made worse by the confidential recital and discussion of
their mental troubles to a suitable person, experience
great relief as a result of this unburdening. Men in the
military hospitals have expressed this over and over

again, in such phrases as, " I have been bursting to tell this to someone who would understand," or, " I have seen many doctors since I left the front, but you are the first who has asked me anything about my mind." Frequently the troubles prove to be caused by their ignorance of the great individual differences in minds, so that the appearance in them of a new but by no means pathological mental phenomenon frightens them unduly. We have already referred to cases of this kind in Chapter I.[1] Another frequent cause of the most intense and continuous mental anguish is the exaggerated self-reproach which the patients attach to some real, but in the judgment of others, comparatively trivial defect or delinquency in themselves. To borrow an expressive phrase, the neurasthenic has " lost his table of values." It is in such cases that a talk with a tactful, sympathetic, broad-minded physician may produce the happiest results.

To assume that one can make the patient forget such worries as these without first discovering what they are, is obviously fatuity at its grossest. Moreover, as we have seen, it is quite insufficient merely to discover that the patient is " suffering from hallucinations " or delusions and then to tell him to dismiss them from his mind. To suppose that, without understanding the nature of and the specific reasons for the development of a particular hallucination, one can " make the patient forget " his interpretation of a real experience which has appealed to him night and day for weeks, or banish a delusion which is gradually becoming systematised and rationalised—*i.e.*, intimately interwoven into the tissues of the whole of his experience—is an assumption which has no foundation in fact.

The point cannot be too much emphasised that many of these patients are quite sane, if conduct be regarded

---

[1] p. 17*f.*

as the criterion of sanity; but they are growing afraid of
the appearance of these abnormal phenomena, and take
them for signs of incipient—or, more usually perhaps, of
established—insanity.   Hence follows the important
corollary that while treatment by isolation has obvious
advantages in certain cases, in the particular group of
patients which we are now discussing it is often dangerous,
for the reasons already emphasised in the last chapter.
The presence of such mental phenomena is usually con-
fided to the physician only after great hesitation, and
such worrying experiences are common in cases of
insomnia and other disorders, which, though troublesome,
do not appear to be grave.   It is therefore possible that
isolation may have serious effects in many cases in which
its net result seems merely to be that the patient is no
better.

It is granted then that in some instances (by no means
all), the patient may be temporarily pained by the
dragging into daylight of the causes of his worry, but it
is usually a case of *reculer pour mieux sauter*.   This
procedure is often inevitable in the medical treatment of
many disorders which have become complicated to any
considerable extent.

We pass now to a difficult task; the consideration of
the moral objections to the procedure of psychological
analysis.   The difficulty obviously lies in the circumstance
that, while in the discussion of the other objections one
could continually point to facts upon which at least, the
great majority of civilised people are in cordial agreement, such unanimity is not so complete upon moral
questions.   Some of the varieties of the moral objection,
however, are not based on such disputable grounds.   For
example, there is the argument that it is bad for the
patient that he should have his inmost mental life dis-
sected and analysed in the thoroughgoing way which we
have described, since it is important for the preser-

vation of his self-regard that, as far as possible, he should consider himself "master of his soul." With the latter sentiment no reasonable person would quarrel. And where it is possible (as it often is) for a slight mental tangle to be straightened out without an extensive and lengthy inquisition, we hold that it is urgent in the patient's interest that his privacy shall be respected. It should be pointed out, however, that since this procedure is equally in the interests of the honest physician—for it will save him time and trouble—it is likely to be adopted wherever possible. In the special military hospitals, for instance, it was often found unnecessary, in mild cases, to press the inquiry very far; the patient "learning his lesson" successfully at an early stage of the proceedings.

But it obviously does not follow that the fact of a man having for very sufficient reasons, admitted the physician into his confidence, must necessarily bring as a consequence a diminution in his self-respect. On the contrary, he often emerges from such an examination with increased confidence and a better opinion of himself, especially if, as so often happens, his self-reproaches have been unfounded. The civilised world contains a relatively large proportion of people who habitually confess their shortcomings to priests. One may recognise that the confessional has its defects, but the assumption that to have recourse to it inevitably promotes mental flabbiness is obviously unfounded. The business man who, when faced with the necessity of successfully meeting an entirely new situation, consults his legal adviser, is not usually blamed for his lack of self-reliance. Conducting one's own legal transactions, like doctoring oneself, may appear (to the vulgar) to show independence, but its results are not always happy.

It is therefore perfectly fair to claim that none of the arguments against the use of psychological analysis have any very great significance. In some cases, however, they express valuable reminders that this delicate and powerful instrument, like all others with these attributes, must be used with care and discretion.

We may now proceed to take stock of our present position and briefly to summarise the contents of the foregoing remarks. Many cases of "functional nervous disorder" or "neurosis" exhibit as their most important characteristics symptoms, the underlying factors of which are demonstrably *mental*. A neurosis may be regarded as the failure of an act of adaptation.[1] The resultant mental disturbances do not seriously affect the "reason" or the "intellect" as was formerly supposed, but are in character predominantly instinctive and emotional. The neurotic's behaviour in the face of an insurmountable difficulty presents a considerable resemblance to that of a child. The reasons why this analogy is not always obvious (though often it is quite plain) is that while in the child one can usually appreciate the cause of the emotional disturbance and watch its progress, these possibilities are often excluded in the case of the civilised neurotic adult. Both his insurmountable difficulty and the historical circumstances which have made it unconquerable may (they do not always) lie within his inmost mental life. Further, the child's difficulty usually is caused simply by his inability to adjust himself to his environment; or perhaps more often to adjust his environment to himself. The adult neurotic, on the other hand, adds to these difficulties the further significant one of a lack of inner harmony. There are warring elements inside as well as outside him: he is trying to fight the enemy with an army which has mutinied.

It follows then that any attempt to restore equilibrium between himself and his social environment must be accompanied by a similar endeavour to bring about his

---

[1] Dr. C. G. Jung's view, *Analytic Psychology*, p. 234.

inner harmony. Therefore, in such cases, a certain amount of psychological analysis is indispensable. Without such investigation the application of physical or psychical methods of treatment must inevitably be a shot in the dark.

The task of psychological analysis is rendered difficult by the fact that not all the motives of the patient's present beliefs, attitudes and actions are conscious; the entry into consciousness of some of the unacceptable motives and memories is obstructed by various mental processes. When the action of these shielding mechanisms has been subverted by various means the real significance and history of the patient's present mental condition becomes clear to him. In the light of this new self-knowledge he begins to cure himself. In a few cases he may require little or no subsequent assistance, but usually a process of re-education[1] is necessary. He may still require to be helped over some of the obstacles which he meets, and he may need more or less frequent encouragement and advice to an extent determined by his disposition, temperament, and character. By these means he is " freed from himself," liberated from the exaggerated emotional tone which has become attached to so many of his memories, and so enabled to face life anew with a harmonious and integrated mind.

The procedure which we have discussed is precisely that which the sensible mother adopts towards a child who exhibits sudden and unreasonable fear, anger, or any socially undesirable emotion. The same method

---

[1]It is of importance to remember that successful re-education utilises the emotional factors in the patient's mental make-up, by helping him to realise the value of the things which will make life once more attractive and worth living. In this process the more the physician knows of the patient's social, moral or religious relations, the earlier and more satisfactory will be his success.

is adopted towards the man who, having muddled his financial affairs, appeals for advice to an experienced and judicious business friend. " Firmness "—of the unsympathetic and unintelligent order—may occasionally produce good results in both these instances, but usually it only makes matters worse. Paying for the commercial muddler a few of his chief debts may remove his embarrassment for the time, but if unaccompanied by an attempt to reform his business methods, the result will usually be merely that such a treatment will enable him to incur fresh liabilities. So it is when a symptom or set of symptoms in a neurosis is unintelligently removed : new troubles frequently break out in fresh places.

We believe that there exist and can exist no serious arguments against the procedure of psychological analysis and re-education which we have just described. But now we come to speak of a procedure introduced during the last few years which has certainly not escaped criticism both of the most flattering and the most hostile kind. This is the method of " psychoanalysis " which we owe to Professor Sigmund Freud, of Vienna, who developed it as an extension and elaboration of the ideas suggested by the teaching he received in France when a pupil of Charcot's.

Perhaps few terms in medicine have aroused so much misunderstanding, so much criticism, well-informed and ill-informed—and so much enmity as this word " psychoanalysis." This latter fact alone, however, should not prejudice the reader for or against it. He will probably remember that it is the exception, rather than the rule, for an innovation to be received without hostility, not only from the general public, but also from experts who work in provinces bordering upon the field in which the new method is introduced.

It should be pointed out that much of the heated discussion which has raged around this word psychoanalysis is due to the fact that the term has different meanings, as used, not only by its enemies, but by its friends. Psychoanalysis, according to Dr. Jung, is a *method;* "a method which makes possible the analytic reduction of the psychic content to its simplest expression, and the discovery of the line of least resistance in the development of a harmonious personality."[1]

Psychoanalysis is therefore a method of psychological analysis. Why, then, have we not used the term psychoanalysis in the earlier part of the book? It was purely to avoid unnecessary and acrimonious discussion on any particular doctrinal aspect of the question which this term may be taken to imply.

It is clear to every thinking person that, in analysing a mental state the physician should use every legitimate means at his disposal. If these means include, as they do, the valuable assistance derived from the study of the patient's dreams, his "associations" whether free or constrained,[2] and other mental phenomena, the doctor may use them freely without thereby subscribing to any one "doctrine of psychoanalysis."

The term psychoanalysis has been widely applied, not only to the diagnostic method, but also to the theories which underlie and determine the subsequent process of re-education. This seems to be a misuse of the useful word "analysis." It may be objected that in all scientific analysis there is some directive hypothesis to be confirmed or disproved, and that in this sense all analysis is based on theory. This is true, but it seems inadvisable to confuse the analytic process with the theory which directs one form of it.

When we come to consider the theoretical presuppositions which underlie the different methods of re-

---

[1] *Op. cit.*, p. 256*f*.
[2] *Cf.* Hart, *op. cit.*, p. 69*f*., Jung, *op. cit.*

education adopted by various physicians, it is not surprising, at this early stage of our knowledge, to discover differences of opinion. The physician will find at every step that in "tidying up" the disentangled functions of the patient's mentality he will need not one theory but many, for his problem is life itself.

All his own human sympathy, with its indispensable basis, a knowledge of his own strength and weaknesses, all his learning in physical science and psychology, all his knowledge of morality and religion must be available for immediate and efficient use. In one interview he may have to lay down the law for the benefit of some ignorant and distressed patient who is desperately anxious to follow his advice unquestioningly; in the next he may be at close grips with a mind more flexible and independent than his own, knowing well that his every little victory must be consolidated, and that every position won may be subsequently counter-attacked by his patient. He must be ready to suggest, discuss, persuade as the time and the conditions indicate.

While, therefore, the ultimate lines on which an ideal diagnostic analysis and curative re-education will be possible are as yet undefined, it would serve no good purpose in a book of this length to raise discussion on the question of psychoanalysis. Its future will be settled, not in the heated atmosphere of the debate, not in the acrid polemics of the correspondence columns, but in the calm, careful examination by the individual worker of his own actual findings and the honest comparison of them with those of others.

# CHAPTER IV.

# Some General Considerations.

IT is instructive to compare the public attitude towards insanity with that adopted in the case of another serious disease, tuberculosis.

There is nowadays a general conviction, not only amongst the medical profession but also amongst a large proportion of the educated public, that tuberculosis is a curable disease. It may exist in a mild and incipient form in many persons regarded as healthy, and, if properly treated in its early stages, with due regard not only to the actual disease in the bodily organism, but also to the healthy environment of the individual, it is almost certainly conquerable. Not many years ago, however, this happy belief did not obtain. A person " in consumption," especially if " consumption was in the family," was regarded as being in a very serious and almost hopeless condition. The patient, shielded from fresh air, inappropriately and insufficiently fed, often succumbed, supplying one more example to support the unscientific conception then prevalent of the inheritance of the disease. But such conditions are passing away. In our medical schools and hospitals special attention is paid to the diagnosis and treatment of early forms of tuberculosis; the importance of preventive measures is emphasised; the influence of the patient's environment in favouring or combating the disease is explained; and

the future medical practitioner is afforded frequent opportunities for personal investigation of tubercular patients.
The old ideas about the "inheritance of consumption" are greatly modified.   No longer is a patient's
disease explained as "in the family" and left at that.
Preventive measures, early treatment, an attempt justly
to appreciate the relative influence of heredity and environment are the watchwords of the modern medical
attack upon tuberculosis.

If, however, we consider the attitude of the general
public in this country towards the malady of insanity
we find a mixture of ignorant superstition and exaggerated fear.   From these there springs a tendency to ignore
the painful subject until a case occurring too near home
makes this ostrich-like policy untenable.   The sufferer
is removed to a "lunatic" asylum, neither himself
nor his relatives being spared the gratuitous extra wrench
to their feelings aroused by this name, which has long
struck terror into the uneducated mind.   He is taken
away by the relieving officer of the district, often under
the pretence of being given "a few weeks in a convalescent home at the sea-side," and eventually finds
himself under lock and key.   Here, as is well known, he
is treated with great kindness.   Neither public money nor
the exertions of the staff are stinted in the effort to
render his lot as pleasant as possible—"the asylum
to-day has become a model of comfort and orderliness."[1]
But the proportion of doctors to patients is on the
average, one to 400, and it is exceedingly difficult to
ensure that all patients, once inside the "lunatic"
asylums, shall be regularly visited by friends from the
outside world.[2]   The attitude of the general public is

---

[1] Hart, *op. cit.*, p. 7.

[2] *Cf.* Dr. Bedford Pierce's statement, (*op. cit.*, p. 43), " I have
met persons otherwise level-headed who cannot be persuaded

not deliberately cruel, but it appears to be far more benevolent than it really is. The community treats the sufferer well, when, *but not before*, he has become a "lunatic." It allows his delusions to become fixed, his eccentricities and undesirable acts to harden into habits, his moods of depression to permeate and cement together the whole of his life—and then interns him and treats him kindly for the rest of his life, but does not give him facilities for gratuitous treatment while he is still sane. *That is the British procedure to-day.*

Lest we should be accused of exaggeration, or worse, we will quote here from published articles and reports.

Dr. Bedford Pierce says:—

"Let me state in a few words the defects of our present system. At present, broadly speaking, no person unable to pay its cost can receive adequate treatment until he is certified as of unsound mind. This practically means that no special treatment is possible until he has utterly broken down, and is so seriously affected as to convince a magistrate that he is decidedly insane. No general hospital will receive such a patient; the public asylums are all closed to any one who begs for protection or treatment, for county asylums cannot receive voluntary boarders even when the cost of their maintenance is forthcoming.

Consequently there is no alternative but to apply to the Poor Law authorities, who, under certain circumstances, provide treatment for a period of two weeks in the workhouse infirmary. The whole system is radically wrong. When the wife of an artisan becomes depressed after confinement, surely it is cruel in the extreme to make her a pauper and send her to the workhouse infirmary, pending a decision as to whether she is insane or no. It is obvious in such a case that this course will not be adopted until the last possible moment, and consequently much valuable time is lost.

---

to enter the grounds of an asylum. Not infrequently all sorts of excuses are made to escape the duty of visiting a relative who is under care, and so real is the danger of neglect that the State has decreed that no order for reception shall be granted without an undertaking that the patient shall be visited at least every six months."

Every practitioner will be able to call to mind patients travelling steadily towards insanity in unfavourable surroundings. This question is brought even more prominently before consulting physicians, especially those interested in nervous and mental diseases." (*Op. cit.*, p. 42.)

In the words of the report of the Medico-Psychological Association :—

"The present system, which compels all persons, except those able to pay adequately for their maintenance, to apply to the Poor Law authorities in order to secure treatment, is unsatisfactory and unjust. In doubtful and undeveloped cases temporary care can be given only in workhouses or Poor Law infirmaries, which, with very few exceptions, lack proper facilities for treatment.
*A system which artificially creates paupers in order to obtain medical treatment necessarily acts as a deterrent, so that too frequently there is serious and even disastrous delay.*"[1]

This is not exactly locking the stable door after the horse has gone: it is double-locking him thoroughly, expensively and often unnecessarily, in someone else's stable.

Let us, for a moment, compare this state of affairs with that existing in the case of tuberculosis. Nobody now believes that the scientific way of treating this disease consists in waiting until the patient has become a positive danger to others, and then locking him up. This point needs no elaboration. But another fact in this connection should not be forgotten. The tubercular patient usually seeks the doctor *of his own free will*, often obtaining treatment in a relatively early stage of the disease.

There are, however, many reasons that deter the mental sufferer from seeking medical help. One of the strongest of these is the wish to cure himself by his own unaided efforts. This is a laudable desire and one

---

[1]p. 5. The italics are ours.

which is extremely helpful and important in mild and uncomplicated cases of relatively recent occurrence, but of which, as we have seen,[1] the gratification is not always possible.  Another factor is the natural disposition which the patient shares with the rest of conventional humanity, to conceal his worries, not only from his friends, but perhaps above all from those of his own household. This tendency to concealment, however, often only aggravates his mental distress.  Particularly is this the case in adolescents.  As is well known, a talk with a kindly, sympathetic and wise person, or even a confession to such an adviser, frequently means the end of many painful mental conflicts.

But in addition to these very natural reasons for deferring recourse to medical help, there are in our own country special causes for delay.  These are due to the prospects imagined by the sufferer to be awaiting him if he discloses his trouble.[2]  The treatment of incipient mental disorder is often a long and complicated process for which the average general practitioner has seldom either the time or the special training.  In very few hospitals in this country is out-patient attendance for such maladies practicable.  For the mental sufferer whose means are not considerable, there exists nothing, if the efforts of the general practitioners fail, but trying to cure himself, or, if he becomes worse, admission to an asylum.  Unfortunately, however, the average asylum, with its one doctor to 400 patients, does not and can not meet his needs.  The successful treatment of mental

---

[1] pp. 77 and 78.

[2] We have in mind throughout the discussion, not the richer members of the community, for whom a relatively expensive holiday or period spent in the nursing home is easily possible, but the great majority of the public, to whom even the ordinary doctor's bill may be a source of financial embarrassment for months or years.

disease usually requires individual care, often lasting over
long periods.   When it is remembered that the asylums
contain a considerable percentage of patients whose
bodily diseases, apart from their mental troubles, require
the doctor's attention, and further, that by the time the
patient reaches the asylum, his disorder has usually
passed through its initial stages, it is easily seen that
our asylum system in its present state—to put it mildly—
is far from conducive to recovery from mental disease.
Considering that, in spite of these drawbacks, 33 per cent.
of the patients are discharged,[1] we can only gladly
recognise the efforts made by the asylums; we are,
however, bound to ask : *What percentage of the
inmates need ever have entered the asylum?* It may
be objected that it is easy, but unfair, to ask such a
question seeing that no satisfactory answer can be given.
To this objection there are two replies: first that,
judging from the present state of affairs, this question
cannot be publicly asked too often; secondly, that
materials for an answer are already forthcoming.   It is
conclusively proved by the experience of other countries
that a large proportion of the patients might have been
cured without being sent into an asylum.   Thus, for
example, in Germany, in the province of Hesse, by
reason of suitable treatment during the early stages of
mental illness the authorities were able to postpone
for ten years the erection of a new asylum.

"The Psychopathic Hospital at Boston, Massachusetts, . . .
was built by the State expressly to deal with recent acute
cases.   No fewer than 1,523 patients were received in its
first year, and of these 590 were received under a temporary
care law, which provides for a week's detention only; large
numbers were also received on a voluntary basis, so that
during the year *48 per cent. of all patients escaped the usual
lunacy procedure.*

[1]R. G. Rows, *Journal of Mental Science*, January, 1912.

On reading the reports of work done, one is struck with the enthusiasm of the medical staff and the vast field of research undertaken.   During  the  two  years  eighteen medical men describe their work covering almost every depart-ment of psychiatry: juvenile crime, tests for feeble-mindedness, incidence of syphilis, alcoholism, hydropathy in its influence on red blood cells, treatment of delirium, prophylaxis, analy-sis of genetic factors, salvarsan treatment, tests of cerebro-spinal fluid, and last, but not least, the value of out-patients' depart-ments and after-care.   There is a special social service depart-ment for the purpose of following up cases in their homes, and it was found that of every 100 admissions 20 needed super-vision on discharge, 24 needed advice, 3 required assistance in arranging their discharge, and 10 showed a need for prophylactic work in their families.

This bald statement of the activities of the Boston State Hospital shows plainly what an important service it renders in providing treatment apart from ordinary asylum associations. It shows how it is possible at such a hospital to organise a medical service which covers all departments of psychiatry; and further, that when the mental symptoms clear up, a patient need not be thrown back into old associations without help or supervision.

This hospital at Boston is but one of many that have been established in the United States in recent years.   Some of the others are due to private munificence; in particular, refer-ence may be made to the Henry Phipps Psychiatric Clinic at Baltimore, the medical staff of which consists of a director, assistant director, a resident physician, two assistants, and five [resident medical officers]. In addition to these are the heads of three research laboratories dealing (1) with clinical pathology and bio-chemical investigation, (2) with neurological research, and (3) with psychopathology."   (Bedford Pierce, *op. cit.*, p. 42.)

In advocating the establishment of separate pavilions for nervous and mental disease in direct association with the general hospitals, Dr. Bedford Pierce says:—

"At La Charité Hospital in Berlin, the visitor enters a small park, and Dr. Ziehen's clinic is but one of many detached buildings devoted to special diseases.   It is as easy and simple for the patient suffering in mind to get advice there as for another with eye and lung trouble."

Let it be noted that none of these German patients, on returning to their relatives and friends, suffer from the stigma of having been to an asylum. In our country some of those same friends during the patient's absence would often have been engaged in "sympathetically" spreading the news of the sufferer's absence and his whereabouts to everybody in the district. To a certain type of mind there is a ghoulish fascination in gloating over the illnesses and afflictions of neighbours. Even though people addicted to such habits may salve their own consciences by exclaiming "poor fellow" at the end of their narrative, the effect of their conduct is none the less brutal and offensive. This is not the place for the discussion of so remarkable and important a phenomenon of social psychology. Nevertheless it plays a great part in the causation of the prevalent dread of treatment for mental disorder.

For many reasons the psychiatric clinic is not regarded by the public as a "lunatic" asylum. In the Giessen clinic in Germany, for instance, both nervous and mental diseases are treated. The patient afflicted with tremor or a paralysed finger visits this institution as well as the sufferer whose troubles if neglected might develop into mental disease. Difficult medico-legal cases resulting from such incidents as those arising from the claims by workmen and others for compensation after accident are sent to this clinic for observation and opinion. "Rest-Cures" and similar treatment are also carried out there. The official title of the institution, displayed at the entrance, is "Clinic for Mental and Nervous Diseases." The institution is therefore regarded by most people in quite a different light from the asylum, and it is not spoken of by the general public with bated breath. One of us, while working in the laboratory of a German psychiatric clinic, was introduced to a visitor who made some remark about "when I was here." To the question, "Were you on the staff, then?" the visitor answered quite naturally, "Oh no, I was here as a patient."

With this experience may be contrasted another incident, this time from our own country. Delegates from a certain Board of Guardians paid a visit to the county asylum to inspect the arrangements made for the comfort of the inmates from their own district. In the next week's local newspaper a report of the visit appeared in the form of the chief delegate's speech at the subsequent board meeting. This report consisted of "funny" stories of the eccentricities of the patients the visitors had seen, and of the delusions from which some of the victims were suffering, with sufficient detail to enable many of the relatives, and possibly some of the friends, of these "lunatics" to identify the afflicted ones. The newspaper account of this humorous effort was punctuated at suitable intervals with "laughter."

It is obviously not claimed that these two accounts are typical either of Germany or of England. But what is claimed is that of these two public attitudes the clinic system promotes the one, the "lunatic" asylum the other.

Before leaving the comparison of insanity with tuberculosis we must remind the reader of some other facts that are important in this connection. We have seen[1] that the scientific study of tuberculosis has materially modified the earlier views concerning its hereditary transmission. It is now held that tuberculosis is not inherited as such; but that a child of tuberculous parentage may begin life with a subnormal power of resistance to the disease and perhaps greater risk of exposure to infection. If later he develops the disease, it is traceable directly to his environment. The corollary is that if his environment be improved, and his body's power of resistance increased

[1]pp. 77 and 78.

meanwhile by all the means in our power, he has a considerable chance of living a life free from the disease. Thus the old pessimistic view is replaced by a distinctly optimistic one.

In the mental disorders that are indubitably traceable to organic disease of the central nervous system, heredity doubtless plays a great role. But two points should be remembered in this connection. First, among asylum patients the number of mental disorders which cannot, *post-mortem*, be traced to organic causes is very great as compared with those that can be so related. For example, of 1,325 patients received at the Burgholzi Central Asylum and University Psychiatric Clinic, Zürich, Dr. C. G. Jung states:—

" . . . in round figures a quarter of our insane patients show more or less clearly extensive changes and destruction of the brain, while three-fourths have a brain which seems to be generally unimpaired or at most exhibits such changes as give no explanation of the psychological disturbance. . . . We must take into account the fact that those mental diseases which show the most marked disturbances of the brain end in death; for this reason the chronic inmates of the asylum form its real population, and among them are some 70 to 80 per cent. of cases of dementia præcox, that is of patients in whom anatomical changes are practically non-existent."[1]

In a great number of mental disorders our present knowledge of anatomy, physiology and pathology is of little help as a means of throwing any light upon the patient's condition. While in no way attempting to belittle the magnificent work in these subjects during the past century, it should be pointed out that its very success has brought about, especially in this country, an unfortunate tendency to regard these methods as the only ones suitable for attacking the problems of insanity. But nothing is more certain than that in the psycho-

---

[1]*Analytic Psychology*, London, 1916, p. 318.

neuroses: hysteria, neurasthenia, psychasthenia and the rest, anatomical and physiological knowledge has not yet passed beyond the theoretical stage[1]. But it is equally indisputable—and the statistics of shell-shock cases have strengthened the evidence for this assertion—that the psychological mode of attack, the treatment of mental disorder by mental means, is now firmly established as a practical method.

It appears, therefore, that precisely in those cases of psychoneurosis which yield to psychical treatment, there is no anatomical, pathological or chemical evidence of inheritance.

But while the contributions of anatomy, physiology and pathology to the treatment of psychoneuroses have not yet gone beyond theoretical and mutually conflicting suggestions, the psychological method of investigation and treatment on the other hand has proved itself of practical use in restoring patients to a normal state of mental health. What scientific justification therefore have we, when considering the action of heredity, for lumping together the organic and the functional mental disorders? The psychoneurosis is often simply a progressive state of mal-adaptation to environment; a mental twist which can be corrected if treated suitably at a sufficiently early stage. Its specific nature is frequently explicable almost entirely in terms of the peculiar educational, family or social relations of the patient's environment. The war has shown us one indisputable fact, that a psychoneurosis may be produced in almost anyone if only his environ-

---

[1] "Everybody agrees," say Déjerine and Gauckler (*op. cit.*, p. 214*f*), "that neurasthenia is a neurosis, *i.e.*, a nervous disease without any known lesions . . . Neurasthenia is due wholly to psychological factors which are essentially, if not exclusively determined by emotion." They then proceed to compare the "materialistic" theories of neurasthenia, showing that they are all still merely speculative.

ment be made "difficult" enough for him.[1]  It has
warned us that the pessimistic, helpless appeal to heredity,
so common in the case of insanity, must go the same
way as its lugubrious homologue which formerly did
duty in the case of tuberculosis.  In the causation of the
psychoneuroses, heredity undoubtedly counts, but social
and material environment count infinitely more.

To some readers the above argument may seem so
obvious as to be superfluous.  To ascribe a patient's
entangled state of mind to heredity without attempting
to discover how far his own personal experiences have
tended to bring about that mental condition, would seem
as fatuous as attributing to heredity the financial muddles
of a son who has inherited from his unbusinesslike
father a badly managed estate.  The trade-adviser called
in to help might for a moment consider the possibility
that the son may have inherited his father's unpractical
character, but surely his first serious efforts would be
to discover where the business methods were wrong or
antiquated and to improve on them.  So it is with the
mental patient; his own history is the important
desideratum.  That of his parents may cast valuable
light upon his trouble, but even then it is often just
because their own difficulties have contributed to the
making of his environment.

One of the most dangerous and misleading terms in
our language is the word "neuropathic;" for it is made
to signify so many things that it ends by meaning nothing.
Etymologically, it should mean "afflicted with disease
of the nerves," a conception the precision of which we
shall discuss below.  Yet on the return from the front
of patients afflicted with "shock" one heard the opinion
at first that the cases were those of "neuropathic" men;
that the soldiers who became affected by shock were

---

[1] Cf. pp. 19 et seq.

weaklings or were descended from mentally afflicted
or nervous parents. It is, of course, unquestionable that
in a large army there must be many soldiers with tainted
family histories; and it is probably equally certain that
such factors play some part in determining the greater
susceptibility of certain men to shock. But it would
be a gross misrepresentation of the facts to label all
the soldiers who suffer from mental troubles as weaklings.
The strongest man when exposed to sufficiently intense
and frequent stimuli may become subject to mental
derangement. It is quite common to find among the
patients suffering from shock senior non-commissioned
officers who have been in the army fifteen or twenty years
(much of which time has been spent in foreign service
under trying circumstances, such, for example, as the
South African War), and have stood this severe strain.
Such men can hardly be called weaklings or "neuropathic."

Even in those cases where there is a definite history
of a neurotic parent, it would be a mistake hastily
to conclude that when the son of such a man or
woman becomes a victim of shell-shock it is due to
heredity. For when the detailed history of such patients
is obtained the fact comes out quite clearly that the
social disturbances in the household of such a nervous
person may be amply sufficient to inflict severe psychical
injuries upon young children.

Further, in many cases the histories themselves clearly
and definitely reveal the real etiology of the mental condition, and point to emotional disturbances in children,
due to the cruelty of drunken parents, a rankling sense
of injustice, a terrifying experience, which may have been
an accident or deliberate maltreatment by some human
being, or again, to the appalling conditions created in
some of these homes by nervous and irritable parents,
as the real trauma which the "shock" has served to
re-awaken.

But when we come to ask *what* disease of the nerves, or, more strictly, of the nervous system, is implied in speaking of the "neuropathic" we find no satisfactory answer. Certainly no one disease is regarded as being the causal factor. And the list of theories is overwhelming. Disturbances of the genital, vaso-motor, or digestive systems, demineralisation, chemical disturbances of nutrition of hepatic or cholæmic origin, visceral ptosis, cerebellar disturbance, thyroid disorder, complex disturbances in functioning of the blood vessels, intoxication, exhaustion[1]: these are some of the numerous theoretical suggestions proposed to account for neurasthenia only. Whether the unfortunate neuropath is supposed to be afflicted by one or all of these is a matter which we certainly cannot decide; for the theories proceed from many different sources.

But we must not lose sight of another important fact in this connection. The neuropathic person's mental troubles, or those at least for which he seeks relief from the physician are by no means in the clouds of theory. They are real enough, and as a rule not to the patient only, but also to his relatives and friends, with whom he finds it difficult to live amicably. Those troubles are based upon fear, anxiety, anger, and excessive curiosity concerning matters about which the normal person would not bother his head. They find expression in outbursts of pugnacity or of unusual self-assertion with its emotion of elation, often followed by self-abasement and subjection, inordinate desires either to be alone or never to be alone, floods of tender emotion, possibly following close on the heels of a mood of blatant self-assertion with no regard for the feelings of others. These relatively simple processes of mind, occurring sometimes in comparative isolation, sometimes inextricably blended or

---

[1] *Cf.* Déjerine and Gauckler, *op. cit.*, p. 214/.

kaleidoscopically transient, are the real marks of the so-called neuropath or neurotic. Bodily troubles may, and often are, added to these. But as every physician knows to his cost (and sometimes to the patient's), and as faith-healers know to their advantage, these bodily diseases are usually exaggerated by the neurotic sufferer, and frequently prove to have but a slight material basis. In other words, the real marks of the "neurotic" are mental.[1]   And one need not be a technical psychologist to see that the above list is nothing but an enumeration of the instincts and emotions possessed in common by ·  all men.[2]

If then, the neuropath is merely displaying instincts which are common to all mankind, what is the difference between him and the normal human being?   The difference is psychologically slight, sociologically immense. While his normal brother reacts instinctively and emo- tionally to his physical and social environment in such a way and to such a degree as to promote his own welfare and that of others, the neuropath does not. Nobody calls the townsman a neuropath who before crossing the street waits on the pavement until the stream of traffic has thinned.   If he did not wait we should rather call him a fool.   But the instinct of fear is largely at the bottom of his so-called intelligent caution—especially if he has ever witnessed a distressing street accident. But what do we say of the man who waits and waits until finally he is too afraid to advance, eventually stealing down to another place so that he may cross in safety?   He is very likely to be called a neuropath.   Or

---

[1]As Professor Kraepelin says, "Nervenkranker sind Geistes- kranker" ("Those 'suffering from nerves' are *sick in spirit*.").

[2]The reader should consult Mr. W. McDougall's ex- cellent treatment of this subject in his *Introduction to Social Psychology*—especially pp. 45-89.

what shall we say of the unfortunate man whose caution
has gone so far that he cannot cross *any* open space
whatever, and is said to be suffering from agoraphobia?

Or again, take the case of a man whose personality,
family or country, is grossly and publicly insulted. If
he strikes at the aggressor, do we call him neuropathic?
But we seldom hesitate to apply this term to the man
who is inordinately touchy, ever on the watch for the
least suspicion of insult towards himself or anything
even remotely connected with him. The emotion of fear
underlies both the attitude of caution and of "funk,"
that of anger, the righteous indignation of the stalwart
and the querulous, peevish irritability of the neurasthenic.
The difference between the behaviour of the normal
man and the neuropath lies primarily in the circumstances
that provoke emotion in them, and secondly in the
violence and duration of the emotion itself.

We should remember also that many varieties of
animals display the kind of behaviour we have described,
and regard as so unusual, if not utterly eccentric, in
our friends. Professor William James reminds us of the
chronic agoraphobia of our domestic cats; and the tamer
of wild animals has good reasons to respect the incessant
touchiness of some species of the genus *Felis*. Do we
invoke theories of visceral ptosis, intoxication and the
rest to explain the behaviour of the average cat or
mule? Scarcely. We say that these animals are actuated
by instinct. Our arrogance makes it difficult for us to
suppose that our suffering human brothers are also
acting instinctively. Yet this is undoubtedly the case.

It has been said of the neurasthenic with aptness and
truth that he behaves like a child. But if a child, normal
in its behaviour up to a certain day, suddenly manifests
fear of being left alone for a moment in a room with
closed doors, or in a street, do we rush for our "Liddell
and Scott" and forthwith proceed to babble of claus-

trophobia or agoraphobia?[1]   Do we follow this up by
solemnly invoking complicated physico-chemical theories
concerning the state of his blood or other bodily fluids?
Finally, do we brand him as "insane" or at least
"neuropathic?"   What we do in this case, if we have
any sense, is carefully to investigate the causes of the
emotional outbreak.   We try sympathetically to understand and re-educate the child to meet such situations
without fear.   In other words, we use a method precisely
similar to that which proves to be of such great use in
treating the psychoneuroses.

The analogy—if it be an analogy and not perhaps an
identity—between the two cases goes still farther.   The
child who manifests extreme fear at "inadequate" causes,
such as we have described, not infrequently agonises
his mother—perhaps soon after his outburst of fright—
by an exhibition of foolhardiness which, if we did not
know of the previous sign of weakness, would cause one
to look upon him as fearless.   In short, the child's fear
is restricted to one or two special situations.   So it is
with many neurasthenics.   Some, for example, may be
driven through traffic in a fast motor car without experiencing the slightest fear, though they cannot bring
themselves to enter an ordinary slow suburban train;
others may surprise us not only by their exhibition of
anger at what we should consider an absurdly slight
provocation, but by their tolerance and self-control in
other (to us) much more annoying situations.   Their
exaggerated emotional reactions are excited not by
general but by specific stimuli; and a little tact, insight
and patience on the part of the physician often reveals
in their past experience, psychological factors which

---

[1]The remarks of Mr. George Bernard Shaw on Max Nor-
dau's "Degeneration" (*The Sanity of Art*, especially p. 88)
might be consulted in this connection,

explain the tremendous personal importance and over-
weighting of these stimuli. If for neuropathic we write:
"unduly hampered by instinct and emotion"—and this
is all we have the right to do[1]—we represent the matter
more truthfully.

Among the laity, before the war, the justification of an
attitude of inertia towards the treatment of mental
disorder (more particularly of the psychoneuroses) was
often based upon two statements. The first was that many
of the phenomena reported were not real, but were the
imaginings of hysterical women. If to this it was
objected that men were not immune to hysteria[2] one was
met by the retort: "But they are 'neuropaths.'" This
war has, however, removed from honest people's minds
the possibility of regarding these phenomena in such a
shamelessly unscientific light. In the military hospitals
there have been hundreds of patients suffering from
psychoneuroses, who are demonstrably neither women nor
neuropaths, in any of the legitimate senses of these terms.
And many of these men have suffered intensely. Their
fears and other emotional troubles are such as they
usually conceal as long as possible, until further endur-
ance is intolerable. Their troubles are real enough to
them. "But they are unreasonable," the healthy philistine
may object. Some (by no means all) of the fears *are*
unreasonable, if by that is meant that the actual danger
(as the healthy man estimates it) and the emotion which
it evokes in the patient are entirely disproportionate.

---

[1]*Cf.* E. Régis, "Les Troubles Psychiques et Neuro-Psy-
chiques de la Guerre," *Presse Médicale*, 23, p. 177, May 27th,
1915.

[2]This term is derived from the Greek word for the womb.
Hysteria was once thought to be due to the wanderings of the
uterus about the body. The term well deserves its place beside
that other ornament of psychological medicine—the word
"lunacy."

But who among us has "sized up" life's dangers so accurately that he can say he knows the precise degree of fear which each one *ought* to evoke?

In some country places the inhabitants to-day are more afraid of the presence in their houses of peacock's feathers or of hawthorn blossom than of scarlet fever. Their fears are unreasonable. But we do not call these people neurasthenics. As a matter of fact, neurasthenia is one of the last diseases likely to attack these rustics. If they vouchsafe any reason for their fear, it is safe to assert that it will be a rationalisation, for its real sources are hidden from them. And if we really wish to discover the cause of their fear we turn for help to the records of folk-lore and ethnology. In other words, we investigate the history of the fear. This history may go back many centuries and the process of recovering it from a series of clues will prove a task of infinite fascination. Now the history of the neurasthenic's fear is likewise obtainable and much more easily, for it is of much more recent date. Its discovery often means the freeing of a mind from torment, the restoration of a useful member to society, and the enrichment of the science whereby other similar liberations may become possible. But how few investigators, as yet, have been attracted by this tremendous untilled field of knowledge!

However, our philistine, while agreeing to this, may, and often does, change his ground. He may add: "When I said that the phenomena were not real I had in mind rather the pains and the paralyses from which the hysteric and neurasthenic suffer—or say they suffer." To this we may answer in the words of Dr. Purves Stewart :—

". . . we must recognise that the neuroses are real diseases, as real as small-pox or cancer. A sharp distinction must be drawn between a hysterical or neurasthenic patient and a person who is deliberately shamming or malingering. . . .

The hysterical or neurasthenic patient usually has no knowledge of the disease which he or she may unconsciously simulate. The various paralyses and pains from which hysterics and neurasthenics suffer are as real to the patient as if they were due to gross organic disease."[1]

There is a view which, while eminently useful and sensible in so far as it concerns neurology alone, is apt, by virtue of these good qualities, to retard the progress of psychical treatment of the neuroses. For it tends to focus the attention of the medical world on their physical basis alone. Such a view is expressed by Dr. Purves Stewart in the manual from which we have just quoted. In his chapter on the neuroses he says:—

"The old definition of a neurosis as a nervous disease devoid of anatomical changes is inadequate. *Disease is inconceivable without some underlying physical basis.*[2] The lesion need not be visible microscopically: it may be molecular or bio-chemical."[3]

Now from the purely material standpoint such a statement is above reproach. But some important reflections occur as one thinks over the paragraph, and especially the statement: "Disease is inconceivable without some underlying physical basis"—as applied for example, to neurasthenia. What are the important signs of disease in the neurasthenic, or what unusual phenomena are there which cause him to seek the doctor? Chiefly, as we have seen on p. 91, the undue dominance in his mental happenings of instinct and emotion. But we cannot say that this by itself is a sign of disease. Otherwise we shall arrive at the paradoxical conclusion

---

[1] *The Diagnosis of Nervous Diseases*, 3rd Edition, London, 1911, p. 355.

[2] Italics ours.

[3] p. 355.

that wild animals, savages and children form the diseased
class *par excellence.*

The behaviour of the neurasthenic differs from that
of the normal person only in degree, and some sane men
might be unhesitatingly regarded as neurasthenic by one
class of society, normal by another.[1]

Moreover, it is perfectly clear that if we adopt any of
the usual views as to the relation between body and
mind, not only disease, but health too is " inconceivable
without some underlying physical basis." Yet of the
molecular or bio-chemical aspects of that basis we know
practically nothing which would help us to understand
even ordinary mental occurrences. So when a normal,
physically healthy mother bursts into tears of joy on her
son's return from the front, is sleepless when she knows

---

[1]This was seen repeatedly in the treatment of the relatively
uneducated soldiers who had become slightly neurasthenic as a
result of the war, especially of those whose life had been spent in
open-air manual work, or in the strict and healthy routine of
the regular army. They complained of emotional irritability,
minor lapses of memory such as the forgetting of relatively
unimportant names or of errands, disturbed sleep, soon
" getting fed up " with their amusements (*e.g.,* " jig-saws," or
billiards for hours every day, month after month in a con-
verted schoolroom or outhouse!). Not only did these phenomena
disturb them, but in a great many cases they seemed to prove
to these unfortunate men that they were insane, or rapidly
becoming so. They would anxiously ask such questions as,
" What is it that makes me so irritable at a slight noise, or
at being brushed against by another patient? I used not to
be like that." Their conduct was also regarded as unusual by
their companions. Now would not the head of a business firm,
an over-worked medical man, a university professor or an army
officer in a position of responsibility, confidently expect to be
allowed *ex-officio* a certain number of these eccentricities without being called " diseased?" But let him drop the privileges
and shelter of his rank, live for a few weeks as a private in
a barracks with a number of high-spirited and thoroughly
healthy soldiers and his behaviour might certainly be considered by them to be queer, if nothing worse.

he is in the trenches, forgets some of her daily duties in perpetually thinking of him, is "on edge" and irritable when she has had no letter from France—though we may be perfectly justified in believing that there are molecular or bio-chemical nervous changes underlying her behaviour, we do not dream of invoking these as explanations of her condition, for of them we know little. Neither do we call her neurasthenic. We understand her condition in that we correctly refer it to the action of instinct and emotion. Its cause is clear to us, and if we attempted to treat it we should know beforehand that the best cure would be the restoration of her loved one, the next best, sympathetic help in facing her worries, the removal of unfounded fears and the production of a serener outlook on the future. In other words, the diagnosis, the tracing of causes, and the treatment would be entirely mental, with no reference whatever to the physical basis, the existence of which we obviously should not deny. Similarly, if a man is troubled by a great moral conflict which produces in him sleeplessness, irritability, abstraction and the rest, the physical basis of his emotional condition may be "materially" treated. His sleeplessness may be reduced by bromides, his irritability and depression by alcohol; but who, if he knew of the great mental conflict, would dare merely to prescribe these?

And this, in the case of many of the psychoneuroses is the crux of the whole matter. The root of the trouble is mental conflict, the complete details of which can seldom be found on the surface of the complex of symptoms. To palliate them one by one is often to provoke new ones. The conflict is sometimes clearly apprehended by the patient, but even then is often jealously guarded from everyone else. Sometimes, however, it is not clearly conscious in all its details, even to him. This is especially the case, if as so often happens, he habitually shuns the thought of it. Faced with an inability to adapt himself to his circumstances, he instinctively relapses into a more childish way of meeting the situation—hence the tears, the irritability, the mental distraction and the rest. This phenomenon, we repeat, is not new. We all acknowledge its existence when we say that the "nervy patient behaves childishly," though perhaps we do not realise what a true conception of the matter we are expressing.

To sum up, while it is indisputable that the psycho-neuroses, like all mental phenomena, have a material basis, we should clearly distinguish between fact and theory in our existing knowledge. Every doctor will naturally seek to make the fullest use of his learning in building up the bodily health of the neurasthenic. But to sit with folded hands and wait for the advancement of our knowledge of microscopic anatomy, physiology or bio-chemistry would be fatuous when there are other and more direct means of treating the numerous and often pathetic cases, which urgently call for cure. The view that "disease, like health, is inconceivable without some underlying physical basis" is sound and useful, but must not be allowed to blind us to the vital significance of the mental factor and its corresponding importance in the diagnosis and treatment of "functional" disease.

It is an indisputable fact that many modern physicians are apt to concentrate their attention almost exclusively upon the bodily ills of their patients. Yet the majority of doctors, especially those who in general practice get to know their patients intimately, admit readily, even eagerly, that not a small number of the maladies which come under their notice are seriously complicated, if not dominated, by mental factors. To take a simple and obvious example, insomnia may be caused by distressing mental conflicts quite as often as by physical disease. The doctor, however, even if he suspects this fact, often hesitates to proceed further in the light of such knowledge.

For this there are several reasons.  In the first place, his arduous, lengthy and expensive medical course has usually never vouchsafed him five minutes' specific training concerning the manifold ways in which human nature may succeed or fail in adapting itself to the complex environment which we call civilisation.  Any wisdom of this kind that he has picked up is due to his own interest and insight in social matters.  The university's contribution to his psychological knowledge usually consists in showing him a handful of comparatively hopeless caricatures of mentality in his short series of visits to the asylum.[1]    It is as if one tried to teach electrical engineering by a few exhibitions of broken-down dynamos, navigation by half-a-dozen cursory inspections of wrecks, finance by a short series of visits to the bankruptcy courts.

The result of this strange conception of medical education is different according to the mental make-up of the particular physician.   There are many whose insight and sympathy enable them to penetrate successfully for some distance into the Cimmerian darkness of the patient's mental troubles.   But do we believe that insight and sympathy alone are sufficient for the successful diagnosis of disorder or disease of the heart or lungs? Mental disorder is subtler, more varied than these, but like them it proceeds along definite lines in definite situations, and it is capable of description even as they are.  It is therefore insufficient even for the talented doctor to rely entirely upon his natural gifts.  But in what other branch of science would it enter his head to do so?

[1]Reform of this state of affairs is urgently needed.  The matter is of such fundamental and far-reaching importance that we have devoted part of the next chapter to the further consideration of its bearings.

But not all doctors happen to be of the type we have described.  There exist many excellent practitioners who are temperamentally so constituted that to them these unaided excursions into the investigation of mental trouble would never suggest themselves.  Predominantly objectively-minded,[1] "without a nerve in their bodies," calm and confident, practical and quick to apply their knowledge in the physical sphere, they have no natural inclination towards the study of such disorders as we have mentioned; and their teachers have too seldom done anything to supplement the exclusively materialistic studies[2] of their medical course.  When, as not seldom happens, he is faced by a case of hysteria or neuras-thenia, such a practitioner is inclined to regard the malady, if it does not prove tractable by rest, change, drugs and diet, massage, electricity, etc., either as "fanciful" and requiring firmness unveiled or veiled,[3] or as the beginning of a lamentable and grave attack of mental disorder.  Unfortunately the number of cases yielding to firmness is not gratifyingly large.  The hysterical patient, too, has a will of his own, and fre-quently proves this fact in a disconcerting manner.  The neurasthenic, knowing long before the doctor tells him, that he ought not to worry, that he ought to "buck up,"

---

[1] "Tough-minded," "matter-mongers," modern writers have called this type, contrasting it with that of the "tender-minded," "reason-mongers."

[2] Of a brilliant teacher of physiology, one who was himself intensely interested in the sciences bordering on his own subject, it was related that when, in lecturing upon the functions of the nervous system in man, he approached difficult problems, he used to say, "But that is a matter for the psychologist." Whereupon the class heaved a sigh of relief and prepared to take notes upon the next subject.

[3] . . . strong electric shocks, cold douches, and other decorous substitutes for a sound birching." W. McDougall, *Psychology*, London, 1912.

frequently becomes acutely critical of his physician, and his powers of judgment are all the keener for their frequent whetting upon his own deficiencies. Not that he should not worry, but *why and how* he should not worry is what he wants to know.

This criticism of the brusque, cheery way in which such a physician may treat mental troubles is not meant to be one-sided or unfair. For some patients, the " firmness " treatment is the right one ; others may be so impressed by the doctor's cheery personality that they recover. But it is safe to say that these are seldom serious cases. The intelligent, highly moral, over-worked business man must not be given the same treatment as the society lady suffering from lack of honest labour— and nobody knows this better than the patient.

This objective way of regarding cases of neurasthenia readily tends on the one hand to make the physician underrate their importance (as when he expects to cure them with " firmness ") and on the other, when they prove impregnable to such attacks, to cause him to exaggerate their seriousness. For, he may argue to himself, if they are beyond cure in this way, what is to be the future of the patients except permanent eccentricity or even insanity? Only a deeper knowledge of the subject can save him from this top-heavy oscillation from unfounded optimism to equally baseless pessimism.

We have noted two of the common obstacles which obstruct the path of the physician anxious to treat mental disorder: his own lack of training and, in not a few cases, his temperamental inclination to look exclusively for visible and tangible material evidence of disease. There is, moreover, at present another serious obstacle consisting in a widespread social convention. This is the unwritten law which commands a person to hide any troubles of a mental nature not only from his friends, but even from his doctor, though he may speak of his physical disabilities to everybody with unblushing frankness. Much could be written on this subject, but the inconsistency of the current attitude has been satirised with inimitable wit and humour by Samuel Butler.

His whimsical fancy has created a civilised country in which this convention does not exist; in which, in fact, the opposite belief obtains. In that land, while a man's bodily ills are counted a disgrace, and not to be mentioned, his mental troubles are regarded as physical illness is with us. The name of that country is *Erewhon*. In *Erewhon*, we are told, physical illness is not only considered shameful but is punishable by imprisonment. Mental trouble, on the other hand, even irritability or bad temper, is regarded as illness requiring the attention of physicians, known as "straighteners." And the consequences of this are that a man will dissimulate the existence of indigestion, giving out that he is being treated for dipsomania, while in answer to questions about his general condition another will quite freely and truthfully say that he is suffering from snappishness. We in England, says the explorer,

"never shrink from telling a doctor what is the matter with us merely through the fear that he will hurt us. We let him do his worst upon us and stand it without a murmur, because we are not scouted for being ill, and because we know that the doctor is doing his best to cure us and that he can judge our case better than we can; but we should conceal all illness if we were treated as the Erewhonians are when they have anything the matter with them; we should do the same as with moral and intellectual diseases—we should feign health with the most consummate art till we were found out. . . ."

This convention inevitably influences the "straightener's" attitude towards his patients, as we are told by the traveller in a description of an interview between his host and an Erewhonian doctor :—

" I was struck with the delicacy with which he avoided even the remotest semblance of inquiry after the physical well-being of his patient, though there was a certain yellowness about my host's eyes which argued a bilious habit of body. To have taken notice of this would have been a gross breach of professional etiquette. I was told, however, that a straightener sometimes thinks it right to glance at the possibility of some slight physical disorder if he finds it important in order to assist him in his diagnosis; but the answers which he gets are generally untrue or evasive, and he forms his own conclusions upon the matter as well as he can. Sensible men have been known to say that the straightener should in strict confidence be told of every physical ailment that is likely to bear upon the case, but people are naturally shy of doing this, for they do not like lowering themselves in the opinion of the straightener, and his ignorance of medical science is supreme. I heard of one lady, indeed, who had the hardihood to confess that a furious outbreak of ill-humour and extravagant fancies for which she was seeking advice was possibly the result of indisposition. 'You should resist that,' said the straightener, in a kind, yet grave voice, 'we can do nothing for the bodies of our patients; such matters are beyond our province, and I desire that I may hear no further particulars.' The lady burst into tears and promised faithfully that she would never be unwell again."

# CHAPTER V.

# Some Lessons of the War.

ARE we, as a nation, doing all that we should for the mentally afflicted? This is the question—no less urgent and important now than it was a century ago—to which we call the serious attention of the reader.

It is no new discovery to recognise the immediate importance of its proper consideration, of the honest facing of the present conditions, and of the urgency for such reform as shall lead to an affirmative answer to our question. Already it has been the subject of considerable discussion in recent medical literature, and in the medical press numerous efforts have been made to bring it to the attention of the general public. In July, 1914, the Medico-Psychological Association of Great Britain and Ireland, a body composed chiefly of the medical officers of our asylums, issued the report of a special committee which had been appointed, in November, 1911, to consider the "status of Psychiatry as a profession in Great Britain and Ireland, and the reforms necessary in the education and conditions of service of assistant medical officers." Unfortunately, within a few weeks of its publication, the outbreak of war prevented that discussion of the question which would otherwise assuredly have followed the publication of so momentous a statement. For in the report stress was laid on the "absence of proper

provision for the early treatment of incipient and undeveloped cases of mental disorder," on the lack of
adequate " facilities for the study of psychiatry and for
research " and upon " the unsatisfactory position of assistant medical officers " in the asylum service. Clearly
the stressing of such points by a committee, thoroughly
competent to form a judgment in such matters, compels
a negative answer to our leading question. The report
makes it perfectly clear that this country has grievously
lagged behind most of the civilised nations in the treatment of mental disease.

Yet all attempts in the way of important and far-
reaching reform have been frustrated, at least during
times of peace, by a strange state of indifference and
inertia and by lack of knowledge. Thus, even so recently
as January 15th, 1916, the *British Medical Journal* was
responsible for the statement " The only hope that our
present knowledge of insanity permits us to entertain of
appreciably diminishing the number of ' first attacks '
lies in diminishing habitual and long enduring drunken-
ness and in diminishing the incidence of syphilis."[1]
This statement would have been sufficiently amazing if
it had been made three years ago; but when the hospitals
of Europe contain thousands of "first attacks" of insanity,
which are definitely *not* due either to alcohol or syphilis,
the only conclusion to be drawn is that its author must
have been asleep since July, 1914, or have become so
obsessed by a fixed idea as to be unable to see the
plain lessons of the war. Syphilis, no doubt, is responsible for a considerable number of cases of insanity, and
drink perhaps for some more[2]; but the incipient forms

---

[1] p. 105.

[2] It should not be forgotten, however, that resort is often
made to alcohol as an easy means of drowning the worry of an
incessant mental conflict. In other words, it is clear that in

of mental disturbance which the anxieties and worries of warfare are causing ought to impress even the least thoughtful members of the community with the fact that similar causes are operative in peace as well as in war, and are responsible for a very large proportion of the cases of insanity. But—and this is still more important—it is precisely these cases which can be cured if diagnosed in their early stages, and treated properly. The chief hope of reducing the number of patients in the asylums for the insane lies in the recognition of this fact, and in acting on it by providing institutions where such incipient cases of mental disturbance can be treated rationally, and so saved from the fate of being sent into an asylum. We may refer the reader to p. 82 *et seq.*, on which was given a short account of the success of these reforms. We reiterate some of the advantages of the clinic system—treatment of the patient without the necessity of the ordinary asylum associations and the consequent social stigma; and the considerable reduction in the number of patients requiring internment in asylums which has followed upon the establishment of the psychiatric clinic.

In this country insuperable obstacles in the way of this urgent reform have been raised by our distinctive national obstinacy, and our blind devotion to such catch-phrases as "the liberty of the subject,"—even when this involves the eventual incarceration of the patient whose liberty to escape treatment and to become insane, is the issue jealously defended. Now, however, the stress of war has compelled us to see matters in another light. The present war, which has been responsible for destroying so many illusions, has worked many wonders in the domain of medicine.

---

treating alcoholism, as in treating insanity, we are not absolved from the plain duty of seeking its mental cause or causes. "Drink" then, in many cases, appears rather as a secondary complication than as a primary factor.

The rational and humane treatment of early cases of mental disturbance has now been inaugurated on precisely those lines which have been so long urged, with such little success, by the more far-seeing members of the medical profession.[1]

A good example of this reform is the splendid work now being carried out, at the Maghull Military Hospitals, near Liverpool, for officers and men, organised and superintended by Major R. G. Rows. The institutions are specially devoted to the treatment of soldiers suffering from "shock" and other psychoses. The success already achieved there is sufficient evidence of the great value of these special hospitals for the treatment of nervous and mental disorders in their early stages.

But if the lessons of the war are to be truly beneficial, much more extensive application must be made of these methods, *not only for our soldiers now, but also for our civilian population for all time.* We have before us the practical experience of those countries which have undertaken this great experiment in preventive medicine, yet apart from the encouraging results of its treatment practised in our special military hospitals, its present position in this country is only too accurately described in the report to which we have referred. With few exceptions[2] "the subject (of mental disease) is left severely alone.[3] Our arm-chair writers direct their attention to safer subjects, such as eugenics, for example, and here they can be happy in feeling they are on secure ground,

---

[1]*Cf.* W. Aldren Turner, *op. cit.*

[2]One of the most gratifying of these is the generous gift of a clinic to London by Dr. Henry Maudsley. Up to the present this institution has been rendering valuable service to the country as part of the 4th London General Military Hospital.

[3]*Appendix to Medico-Psychological Association Report,* p. 18.

because they are aware that their neighbour knows little more about it than they do. Or they inspire reports, and I quote a sentence from a recent report as a contrast to the encouraging sound of the word 'recovering.'[1]

In the *Standard* newspaper a few days ago, (*i.e.*, in 1914) there was a reference to a report issued by the London County Council in which one paragraph began with the statement, 'Once a lunatic, always a lunatic.' This is the message sent in this country to our sufferers, a message as brutal as it is unjustifiable. Again, in the *Standard* of February 11th in the year of grace 1913, there appeared the statement that 'the Camberwell Guardians have issued instructions that the use of "anklets" on violent lunatics in their institutions is to be discontinued.'"

With reference to the dictum "Once a lunatic always a lunatic" we should like to call attention to another statement in this report. " The fact that, *even under the present conditions of delayed treatment, about 33 per cent. of those admitted to the asylums of England and Wales are discharged recovered*, demonstrates that the feelings of helplessness and hopelessness, with which such illnesses are usually regarded, are by no means justified. The evidence of many authorities who have had practical experience of the value of treatment during the incipient stages of the illness, shows conclusively that the exercise of scientific care during the early phases of mental disorder would save many from such a complete breakdown as would necessitate certification and removal to an asylum. In all other branches of medicine facilities for dealing with disease in its initial stages are recognised as indispensable and

---

[1] " One thing which impressed . . . [us] . . . when going through . . . the Giessen clinic with Professor Sommer, was the frequency with which we heard him utter the word 'recovering' as we passed the patients." *Ibid*, p. 17.

therefore the Committee regard it as essential that, in the
large centres of population at any rate, means should be
provided to obviate the delay that now exists in providing
adequate treatment for mental disorders. It is, therefore, recommended that psychiatric clinics should be
established."[1]

Again, at the International Congress of Medicine in
London, in August, 1913, an important discussion of
these problems was introduced by an account of the
Henry Phipps Psychiatric Clinic which has been established in Baltimore for the treatment of mental disorders,
and for teaching and research in this subject. In the
course of the discussion special emphasis was laid upon
" the necessity for *teaching the medical profession and
the public* that many mental disorders are absolutely
recoverable, that good hospital and scientific treatment
save many, that the mere economy of our monster institutions represents a sham economy paid for by the patients
and their families, and that psychiatry must extend
beyond the asylums."[2]

Emphasis was also laid upon the importance of making
these hospitals, for the care and cure of those suffering
from mental illness, centres for scientific education and
research and for the development of prophylactic
measures. For, unless medical students are provided
with facilities for the study of these early cases the
present deplorable condition of affairs will be perpetuated.
All honest medical work is essentially research; for every
individual patient presents problems which need investigation; and facilities should be provided for making
such enquiries under the most favourable conditions. As
Dr. Flexner has well said,[3] it is impossible " to develop

[1] *Op. cit.*, p. 2.
[2] *Op. cit.*, pp. 15-16.
[3] *Vide infra.*

two types of physician, one to find things out, the other to apply what has been ascertained. For the same kind of intelligence, the same sorts of observation, knowledge and reasoning power are needed for the application as for the discovery of effective therapeutic procedure."

This last consideration leads us to the examination of another potent factor in the present situation, *viz.:—*

*The Attitude of the Medical Profession.* When it is remembered that mental factors play an important rôle in the causation and continuance not only of obviously mental disorder but also of bodily troubles, and that therefore successful diagnosis and treatment must inevitably take these factors into account, it may seem remarkable that the medical profession as a whole should take so little interest in, and know so little of psychology. Even when the psychological aspect of their problems becomes the outstanding element in diagnosis and treatment, the vast majority of medical practitioners show little or no inclination to satisfy their scientific curiosity and to endeavour to understand the condition of their patients.

But this attitude becomes more comprehensible, and in a certain measure more excusable, when we look into the courses of instruction provided for students in our medical schools. What training in psychiatry—to say nothing of psychology and psychopathology—have they received in the schools? How many hours have been spent in lectures or demonstrations upon mental diseases? And how has this modicum of time been spent? How many hours are devoted to actual *personal investigation* of patients suffering from early mental disorder? All the instruction in such matters that our students get at present in most of the medical schools is given in a few hours during one term, when they visit an asylum where demonstrations are given of *advanced* cases of mental disease: "melancholia," "mania," "dementia," etc.

Lest we may be accused of wild statements, let us quote again from the Medico-Psychological Association's report. (The italics are ours.):—

"... the attention given to mental diseases before qualification is much less than that given in many other countries. Owing to the absence of clinics, the medical student *has no opportunity of observing borderland or undeveloped cases.*" (p. 6.)

"To this absence of teaching facilities is due the lack of knowledge of the general practitioner, who should be competent to recognise, and possibly to deal with, some of the earliest symptoms; *to this we owe the lack of real equipment in those who enter the lunacy service.*" (p. 21.)

In this connection it is interesting to quote from a comparatively recent report on medical education. Four years ago the Carnegie Foundation for the Advancement of Teaching published a report on "Medical Education in Europe." This work was remarkable both for its perspicacity and thoroughness and for the frankness and detachment with which its author, Dr. Abraham Flexner, expressed the opinions he had formed after a detailed study of the medical schools of this country and on the Continent. This valuable and important document was barely noticed by the medical press in this country. But this is not the place for a discussion of the psychology of this conspiracy of silence. For it certainly does not imply any reflection upon the impartiality or the thoroughness of Dr. Flexner's research; on the contrary, it is a silent tribute to the seriousness of the exposure of the weaknesses of our medical schools. But the report is also a most valuable appreciation of the strength of our methods of medical education. It provides a minute analysis and comparison of the methods of teaching clinical medicine in Great Britain and on the Continent. The summary clearly defines the distinctive merits of the British system, and has such an important bearing upon the questions we are considering in this book that we will quote its most essential paragraph.

" The limitations by which medical education in Great Britain is hampered have now been candidly exposed. It is nevertheless true that in respect to the student, nowhere else in the world are conditions so favourable. In our discussion of Germany we pointed out that its clinical instruction was overwhelmingly demonstrative; that the student *saw* and *heard* but almost never *did*. Clinical education in England has completely avoided this wasteful error. It is primarily practical. It makes, indeed, the huge mistake of assuming that a more scientific attitude towards the problems of disease is in some occult way hostile to practicality; for it protests against the adoption 'of modern methods of investigation, as though practical teaching would be in some inexplicable fashion endangered thereby. However, that may be, the English are indubitably correct in holding that sound medical training requires free contact of the student with the actual manifestations of disease. It is the merit of English and, as we shall also perceive, of French medical education that the student learns the principles of medicine concurrently with the up-building of a veritable sense-experience in the wards, and that he acquires the art of medicine by increasingly intimate and responsible participation in the ministrations of physician and surgeon. The great contribution of England and France to medical education is their unanswerable demonstration of the entire feasibility of the method of instruction which the end sought itself imposes."[1]

We have quoted at length this vivid and accurate portrayal of the distinctive feature of British methods of clinical instruction in order to emphasise the fact that in the teaching of psychological medicine the British utterly neglect this excellent method of instruction which Dr. Flexner considered so admirable a feature of our medical schools. The British method of teaching psychological medicine, so far as the subject is taught at all,[2] is that of class-demonstration, but, as we have

---

[1] p. 202.

[2] " . . . at present we have few facilities for teaching the

seen, the avoidance of exclusive reliance upon this method is the feature on which Dr. Flexner congratulates the British schools. On the other hand, while the Germans are criticised for their adherence to the class-demonstration, it should be remembered that, although this source of weakness appears in their undergraduate classes, it is they and not we who provide facilities, in their clinics, to the post-graduate student for free contact with patients in incipient stages of mental illness.

Therefore we have neglected to apply, in the case of mental diseases, the very methods which in all other branches of medicine have been so conspicuously successful as to be selected by an impartial critic as the distinctive merit of British medical training.

We have indicated briefly the type of instruction in psychiatry obtaining in our medical schools at present. Its educational value is certainly very slight; and—what is worse—it serves to give the future doctor a hopeless outlook on insanity. For the instruction of students in the nature and treatment of tuberculosis we do not send them to some sanatorium to gaze upon patients dying from the disease. They personally examine patients in the early stages and learn to recognise the subtler manifestations of the onset of the tubercular attack, when there is some hope of giving useful advice and saving the sufferer. Why cannot mental disease be dealt with in the same way? Why cannot our students be afforded, in general hospitals, the opportunity of personally examining patients in the incipient stages of mental disturbance? They would then not only acquire a knowledge of the real nature of insanity, but would also learn, in the school of experience, the individual differences which are exhibited in the working of the normal mind, a lesson

---

subject, and the subject is not taught." (*Medico-Psychological Association's Report*, p. 20.)

which would be of the utmost value to them in dealing with *all* their patients, whether their ailments be bodily or mental. But in addition such a training would impress on them, in a way that nothing else could do, the vitally important fact that mental disease is curable, and is not the hopeless trouble which is likely to be suggested by the spectacle of a few asylum patients in advanced stages of lunacy.

Even, however, if the asylums afforded better facilities for the proper study of mental disease than unfortunately is the case in most institutions in this country, they are usually not sufficiently near the medical schools to permit the student properly to acquire his knowledge, as he does of other diseases, by frequent and regular attendance for a considerable period of time. Nor, as yet, have many of the medical officers in our asylums sufficient up-to-date knowledge of psychiatry to enable them usefully to co-operate with the medical schools and the teaching staffs of the general hospitals in achieving the desired aim. We know that there are some exceptions to this general statement, and fortunately they are becoming more numerous. But viewing the condition of affairs in the country as a whole, in respect of this important matter, one can only accurately describe it as deplorable. These are hard words, and we are well aware that their use may expose us to the charge of superficial, uninformed and even spiteful criticism. Let us, therefore, turn to the gratifyingly frank and honest statements of the asylum workers themselves, embodied in the report from which we have quoted.

"*The tendency of routine to kill enthusiasm and destroy medical interests.*

The promotion or advancement of a medical officer depends so little upon his knowledge of psychiatry that he has no inducement for that reason to devote himself to an earnest study of the subject. His work is apt to begin and end with the discharge of essential routine duties to the exclusion of careful clinical and scientific investigation.

The work assigned to junior medical officers is, in the majority of cases, monotonous, uninteresting and without adequate responsibility. For those whose personal enthusiasm keeps alive in them the desire to extend their knowledge, such opportunities as that of study-leave are rarely afforded them. The existing system, therefore, leads to the stunting of ambition and a gradual loss of interest in scientific medicine. It tends, therefore, to produce a deteriorating effect upon those who remain long in the service."[1]  (pp. 8 and 9.)

## Methods of Making Appointments.

"Appointments are made by lay committees, which, though they are generally wishful to appoint the best candidate, are in most cases without expert advice, and without adequate knowledge of the factors involved. The results are, therefore, generally haphazard in character, often dependent upon influence or personal consideration, as they frequently bear but little relation to the actual claims and qualifications of the candidate." (p. 7.)

We submit then, that our expression of opinion is but a paraphrase of the authorised report. The study of this publication as a whole will only deepen this impression in the reader.

In the foregoing paragraphs we have pointed out the vital importance of research in relation to mental disease. All properly conducted clinical work is of the nature of original investigation; and in the examination of patients suffering from mental disturbance this is particularly the case. But a vast amount of research work must be

----

[1]Concerning this sentence the *British Medical Journal* wrote, on Nov. 29th, 1914, "A more severe indictment of the existing system than is contained in this report it would be difficult to frame . . . We can add nothing to this strongly worded condemnation except an expression of agreement with the opinion that the statement of the facts submitted demands the earnest attention of public authorities and all interested in the welfare of the insane."

carried out in properly equipped hospitals and laboratories
if we are to deal with the problems of lunacy in the same
efficient manner as we have learnt to treat tuberculosis.
In this connection it is important to emphasise the lack
of an adequate knowledge of normal psychology
among many of the medical officers and the absence of
psycho-pathological research in so many of our asylums.

It must not, however, be inferred that the only reform
needed is an increase and improvement of the *mental*
treatment of mental disease. It is not merely the psychological side that is neglected. The most depressing
aspect of the present state of affairs *is the comparative
absence of all research..* Investigations into the material
basis of mental disease, while certainly more numerous
than psychological investigations, are at present few in
number. Hosts of problems concerned with the nervous
system are awaiting investigation, and the admirable
results obtained by the small band of energetic workers
in our country serve to show how sadly our nation is
neglecting its golden opportunities for accomplishing
much more in this respect. Important problems in connection with the normal and morbid anatomy of the
nervous system, its pathology and its bio-chemistry,
suggest themselves to the worker at every step. The
physiological and psychological effects of different diets,
of drugs like the hypnotics, *et cetera*, how little we know
of them! Are we to rest content in leaving this vast
unknown land to be charted by other nations?

Original research is thus urgently needed in all those
departments which should be included in asylum work.
But it is also necessary for the researches to be co-
ordinated. Not a few individual doctors in our asylums,
usually members of the junior staffs, are endeavouring
to carry on original investigations; but in the majority
of cases the absence of any prospect of direct or
indirect personal benefit from this work damps their

enthusiasm, if it does not make such work wholly impossible. And, of course, without the willing co-operation of the asylum authorities co-ordinated researches cannot be carried out.

We shall again quote from the report of the Medico-Psychological Association in justification of our statement:—

"Research is largely dependent on individual enthusiasm, but can certainly be stimulated and maintained by the co-operation of the senior medical staff. There is reason to fear that such work is undertaken in some quarters without any guidance or encouragement from seniors, and laborious original investigations have received little or no recognition from those in authority . . . Although there is no uniformity of practice, report is made that in many asylums junior medical officers are placed in charge of chronic cases only, and have no duties in reference to the treatment of newly-admitted cases. This appears to be most undesirable. Junior medical officers, in addition to their statutory routine duties, should be given the opportunity of co-operation with their senior colleagues in clinical work. Consultation between the various members of the medical staff in doubtful and interesting cases is very desirable . . ." (p. 30.)

If the reader will pause for a moment, and in imagination put himself in the position of a junior medical officer, "*placed in charge of chronic cases only*," he will not only come to understand the "stunting of ambition and the gradual loss of interest in scientific medicine" of which he has read, but may admire the self-restraint of a report which can speak in temperate language of such a state of affairs.

Another difficulty that stands in the way of this urgently needed reform in medical education is the inadequacy of the text-books available for the student. In many of these text-books the introductory chapters contain some, often irrelevant,[1] morbid anatomy, and the

---

[1]Irrelevant because such books give an account of the morbid anatomy of the nervous system only as it presents itself after disease of very long duration.

remainder deals with "psychology." The latter frequently consists largely of anecdotes, often "funny" and sometimes more appropriate to the "after-dinner" hour than the text-book, and enumerations of the mental *symptoms* of the cases. In practically every available English text-book the latter are depicted only as they appear after they have become fixed, habitual, hardened and rationalised. Such "units" of terminology as "delusions," or "delusions of persecution," "hallucinations," etc., are freely used. In other departments of clinical medicine the text-book writer does not describe a patient as suffering from a cough, and leave it at that; yet the phrase "suffering from delusions" is the veriest commonplace in the text-books. Yet just as a cough may be due to tuberculosis of the lung, pharyngeal irritation, hysteria, or a variety of utterly different causes, each class of case requiring a different treatment, so the causes of delusions are even more infinitely varied.

But the gravest defects of these text-books is that few of them make any attempt whatever, except in the case of such forms of disease as have an organic cause, to explain the *development* of the trouble, the precise nature of the primary cause or causes and the way in which the disturbance of the patient's personality has been gradually effected.

Unfortunately there are serious defects in many of the works upon general psychology which render them almost useless to the student of psychological medicine. This may explain, if it does not excuse, the quaint selection of subjects, often wholly irrelevant or inappropriate, which form the contents of the psychological section of many English books on mental disorders. But this deficiency is not a sufficient excuse for the neglect of the kind of instruction that is of vital importance for the proper understanding of such disorders. When books such as those written by McDougall, Stout, Hart, Shand,

and Déjerine and Gauckler, are available, it is possible to use the facts of normal psychology as the natural, rational and necessary means of explaining and interpreting departures from the normal state.

We may summarise here some of the chief defects of our national system of treating mental disorder. First and foremost is the serious waste of time which almost invariably occurs before the mental sufferer comes under medical care. This is due to a variety of causes—all of them preventable.[1] The chief is that, lying in the path of patients who would *voluntarily* seek help, there is the insurmountable obstacle of the asylum system and its restrictions. The men in the asylum service, who have the opportunity of acquiring an intimate knowledge of mental diseases, are *forbidden* to carry that knowledge into the outside world for the benefit of the mental sufferer. If a patient, suffering from a mental disorder in its earliest and easily curable stage, should voluntarily go to an asylum and ask for advice, all that can be done for him is to suggest that he should consult a medical man outside, or to recommend him to call and see the relieving officer. Now, unless the patient has considerable means, it is practically certain that he will be able to consult no medical man who is conversant with—much less expert in—the treatment of early mental disorder. And, though the relieving officer's intentions may be of the best, it is just his 'help' and all that it means, that the unfortunate is so desperately striving to avoid. In short, all that the officials under our present system can say to such a man is, "Go away and get very much worse, and then we shall be allowed to look after you!" Can stupidity go farther than this?

Even, however, if the doctor were allowed to help such a person in the asylum, this would be far from an ideal solution of the difficulty. Entry into such an

[1] See "The Reform of Mental Treatment," *Athenæum*, June, 1917.

institution, even if voluntary, would entail the serious
social stigma which has been so often mentioned. Furthermore, the asylum, with its associations and implications,
particularly the assumption of the irresponsibility of the
patients interned in it, would destroy one of the chief
therapeutic agents in the treatment of such cases. We
mean the conviction of the patient that he is still responsible for his actions, and that he is still able, under
direction, to cure himself.

The place to which such a patient should be able to
go is obviously one which is exempt from any stigma;
one in which of his own free will he may stay for a time
under care, or if this be unnecessary, as is very frequently
the case, which he may visit at frequent intervals for
advice and treatment. It should be staffed by skilled
specialists who are familiar with the diagnosis and treatment of *early* and *incipient* mental disorder, not only
with that of advanced insanity. For years such institutions
have existed in other countries and form an important
part of their contribution towards the alleviation of human
suffering.

The chief functions of such a clinic would be :—

(1) Attendance on the mentally sick.

(2) The provision of opportunities for personal intercourse between patients and the psychiatrists in training.

(3) The theoretical and practical instruction of students.

(4) Advising general practitioners and others who are
faced with difficult problems arising in their daily work.

(5) To serve as a connecting link between investigation in the large asylums and that in the anatomical,
pathological, bacteriological, biochemical, psychological
and other laboratories of the universities.

(6) The scientific investigation of the mental and bodily
factors concerned in mental disease.

(7) The furtherance of international exchange of scientific knowledge concerning mental disorder, by the welcome accorded to visitors from other countries.

(8) The dissemination of medical views on certain important social questions and the correction of existing prejudices concerning insanity.

(9) When necessary, the after-care of the discharged patient.

We have already given some details of the activities of a few of the clinics abroad[1] and have pointed out their valuable function in saving a high percentage of patients from the fate of an asylum, while at the same time relieving the community of the serious expense of keeping these patients for life as pauper lunatics.

We may quote from an article by Dr. R. G. Rows[2] describing the psychiatric clinics at Munich and Giessen:

"They are carried on upon the lines of 'freely come, freely go,' as far as is consistent with the safety of the patient and of the public. In neither of these clinics is any legal document necessary for the admission or discharge of patients. But where the character and severity of the mental disturbance require the longer detention of the patient in the clinic or in an asylum, such detention can be exercised only under a legal procedure which carefully safeguards the rights of the patients.

In this way it is possible to avoid the stigma which is attached to certification and seclusion in an asylum. That this is appreciated by the general public is demonstrated by the number of people who make use of the opportunities offered them. To the clinic at Giessen, with its seventy beds, between three and four hundred patients were admitted in 1907. From the report of the clinic at Munich for the years 1906-7 we learn that there were 1,600 admissions in 1905 (the first complete year after it was opened), 1,832 admissions in

[1] pp. 82 et seq.

[2] "The Development of Psychiatric Science as a Branch of Public Health," Journal of Mental Science, January, 1912.

1906, and 1,914 admissions in 1907. At the present time admissions go on at the rate of ten or twelve per day. It should be mentioned that at Munich the clinic is open night and day for the reception of patients, so that they can be brought under the care of an expert at the earliest possible moment, and the painful impressions produced often by detention and restraint by unskilled persons and unsuitable surroundings are reduced to a minimum. This immediate treatment at the hands of men experienced in insanity is a matter of the greatest importance, from the point of view of a favourable termination of many of these cases.

Let us now consider the actual treatment of those admitted into these institutions. What most strongly impressed us in these clinics was the absence of noise and excitement amongst the patients; it was certainly an ample demonstration of the value of the means of treatment adopted. It is recognised in the first place that patients must not be crowded together: none of the wards contain more than ten beds . . . For the patient who is too excited to be kept in bed or who disturbs the others too much, experience has shown that prolonged warm baths provide the best means of quieting him and bringing him into such a condition as will allow of his being kept in the ward. The extent to which the bath treatment is employed may be judged from the fact that besides the baths used for ordinary purposes of cleanliness there are in the clinic at Munich eighteen baths for prolonged treatment, five movable baths, one electric, and one douche bath. The wet pack is occasionally used. The baths are so arranged that the patient can remain in the bath for days or weeks as the case demands, sleep there and take his food there. The result of the treatment is that hypnotic drugs and confinement to a single room have come to be regarded as evils to be used only on rare occasions; in fact, the single rooms are occupied by convalescent and quite quiet patients and not by recent and acute cases.

Treatment on these lines will of course necessitate the employment of a large medical and nursing staff. At Giessen, with 70 beds and between three and four hundred admissions a year, there are five medical officers including the director. At Munich, with one hundred and twenty beds and three or four thousand admissions, there are fifteen medical officers to carry on the work of examination and supervision of the patients. The nursing staff must be provided in the proportion of at least one to five. This is of course a high figure, but there are two conditions to be remembered: first, the very large number of admissions dealt with, and secondly, that these clinics are established not for the housing of the insane, but for the care and cure of those suffering from incipient mental disturbances—a most important distinction, and one not yet fully appreciated in this country.

Besides the patients admitted into the clinics for treatment, a large number obtain advice and help from the out-patients' department."

It should be mentioned that in Germany there is a psychiatric clinic attached to every university.

Among the most important functions of a clinic are instruction and research. Each assistant in the Munich clinic carries on some chosen line of study. In order that he may have better facilities for becoming acquainted with the literature on the subject and finishing his selected work, he is given, besides his annual month's leave, two months of each year for this purpose. Frequent evenings are set apart for discussions of original work carried on in the clinic and elsewhere. Besides this, numerous short courses in special subjects are provided, so that it is possible to enter the clinic for instruction in matters requiring a special knowledge of delicate technique and diagnosis.

Of very special importance in the Munich clinic is the course for qualified medical men. In 1907 this was attended by *sixty men, of whom one third were foreigners*. What can we, in Great Britain, show in comparison with this? Our physical, chemical, physiological, and pathological laboratories attract distinguished foreigners from the universities of other countries, though twenty would be a number on which even our most celebrated laboratories would pride themselves. But how many foreigners come to us to study insanity? Very few indeed, and the reason is not far to seek.

In the Munich clinic, again, we find well equipped rooms for clinical examination, for the deeper investigation of mental life by experimental psychology, for the study of morbid anatomy and pathology and for the finer examination of the blood and other fluids of the body. Furthermore, these laboratories are not only spacious and well-equipped, but are occupied by busy, keen and skilled workers. Testimony to their activity is afforded in abundance by their frequent publications.

We submit, then, that the clinic system is a decided advance in the treatment of mental disorder which other countries have adopted while for years we have stood by with folded hands.[1] From the humanitarian and the scientific point of view there is everything to be said in favour of the clinic. The practical Englishman will, however, ask " What about the financial aspect? Are not these institutions, with their heavy proportion of doctors and nurses to patients, prohibitively expensive? "

The answer to this question is that certainly the clinic is relatively more expensive than the asylum. But since the function of the clinic is to save as many patients as possible from entering the asylum, it is obvious that its expense must be judged from a special standpoint. The maintenance of a repair shop is always comparatively costly, whether the material to be mended be human or not. The cost per day of repairing a motor car is usually distinctly higher than the daily charge for garaging it in its broken-down state. Yet we gladly pay the higher charge for the simple reasons that a motor car in its garage is of no use to us, and that the daily charge for housing the car would amount to a colossal figure if paid for many years. Cannot we apply the same reasoning to

---

[1] The gratifying establishment of the Maudsley clinic and the provision of facilities for out-patient treatment at a few hospitals in England and Scotland are signs that matters are at last improving. But we are sure that the physicians in charge of such out-patient departments would be the first to admit their inadequacy and to urge the desirability of the psychiatrical clinic of the kind described in this book.

the case of the mentally disordered human being? This
is to take the very lowest view of the value of the
individual to the community. Yet it would seem that the
British public, so far, has been impervious even to this
financial consideration.

But, it may still be asked, cannot the doctors in the
asylums carry out the work suggested? The answer to
this is, that apart from the undesirability of allowing a
patient suffering from a mild mental disorder to be
associated with an institution housing the definitely insane,
it is a physical impossibility for the asylum doctors to do
this work so long as the present proportion of doctors to
patients remains unchanged. How many members of
the British public realise the fact that it is quite usual
for an asylum doctor to be in charge of at least 400
patients, and that this number sometimes rises to
600? When it is remembered that insane patients are
even more prone than the average person to suffer from
physical ailments, and that their mental disorders are
infinitely complicated by the delay incurred before they
come under medical care, it becomes clear that the
doctor who would succeed in treating such patients
individually would require titanic energy and the addition
of at least twenty-four more hours to each of his working
days. We cannot therefore compare the staff of a clinic
with that of a British asylum, for the staff of the latter
is lamentably and obviously too small.

Regarding the financial aspect of the question we may
quote again from Dr. Rows' article :—

". . . we shall no doubt be met with the objection that the
provision of such institutions will involve the expenditure of
such an immense sum of money. I believe we spend in
Great Britain about £3,000,000 a year on those suffering from
various forms of mental affliction. That, certainly, is an
immense sum to spend while getting so little in return. A
large proportion of this money is spent in housing, feeding,
clothing, and taking care of the 97,000 inmates of the county

and borough asylums of England and Wales. We learn from the commissioners' report, published in 1910, that 20,000 patients were admitted into these asylums during the previous year, and of these, over 30 per cent. were discharged after a longer or shorter detention. Now it may safely be said that very few of these 20,000 fresh admissions did obtain, or could have obtained, any advice for their mental illness at the hands of anyone who had had experience of mental disorders, before they reached the stage when certification and seclusion in an asylum became necessary. When we visited Giessen we were informed by Professor Sommer that in the province of Hesse, by reason of suitable treatment during the early stages of mental illness they had been enabled to postpone for some years the erection of a new asylum in the province. Is it not therefore fair to assume that, if facilities were provided whereby expert advice and treatment in a well-organised psychiatric clinic could be obtained by those threatened with a mental breakdown, we should save enough of the £3,000,000 to justify the expenditure involved in the establishment of such clinics? Further benefits would be derived from them in that we should be able to avoid the breaking-up of the home, which now, in so many instances, follows the removal of the bread-winner of the family to an asylum and his long detention there."

And

". . . it may be suggested that we should attempt to demonstrate the possibility of saving money in order to carry the public with us in the matter. I do not think that is necessary. The value of treatment of the early stages of mental disorder cannot be expressed in pounds, shillings and pence. Moreover, I submit that our duty as medical men is to guarantee the satisfactory treatment of the patient, and we have no right to allow our action to be dominated by monetary considerations. I feel sure that the more this question is placed before the public in an intelligent manner, the more we insist upon the necessity for early treatment and for scientific knowledge as a basis of any treatment, the less will the public grumble about expense. We have ourselves to thank if the public refers so constantly to money matters. Do we ever encourage the public to regard the question from any other point of view? Do we point out that insanity is a product of civilisation? Do we encourage people to regard insanity as an illness for which something can be done and which should be treated with intelligent and humane consideration? Do we not rather say with the public, "Lock him up, put him where he can neither harm himself nor his neighbour?' Do we not talk of sterilising the unfortunate sufferers and preventing marriage and procreation before we have made an honest effort to investigate what insanity really is, what is the mechanism of its production, and how we can teach those so afflicted to help themselves? How then can we expect the public to do anything but grumble at the expense? The public has not objected to spend money in other branches of medicine when the necessity has been demonstrated, and there is no reason, if the members of the lunacy service in this country will develop confidence in themselves, why they should not be able to instil confidence into those outside the profession."

*Suggested Reforms.* After the depressing picture of the present state of affairs in this country it will be asked, "What should be done to remedy it?" The answer to this question is clear and definite.

For the relief of the mentally afflicted amongst us, and especially for the prevention of insanity, it is our bounden duty as a nation to take measures such as most civilised countries have adopted some time ago. For this purpose it is necessary that there should be hospitals to which patients in the early stages of mental disturbance can go, without any legal formalities, and receive proper treatment from physicians competent to diagnose their troubles and to give them appropriate advice. It is important that such special hospitals should be attached to general hospitals, so that sensitive patients may not be deterred from resorting to them by the fear of the stigma which in this country, unfortunately, is so inseparably linked with the idea of a "lunatic asylum." It is also important that such institutions should be affiliated to medical schools, not merely to ensure the adequate education of the coming generations of medical practitioners, but also to afford the staffs of such hospitals the proper opportunities for carrying on the work of investigation which is essential for the success of the scheme we have sketched out.

No less important and urgent a reform than the foregoing, however, is another consideration—the *legal* aspect of the treatment of the mentally deranged.

The glaring defects of the present system have been well and briefly pointed out by Dr. Bedford Pierce in his article from which we have quoted, published in the *British Medical Journal* of January 8th, 1916.

Again, Sir George Savage, writing in Allbutt's *System of Medicine* (Vol. VIII, p. 429) states :—

"The lunacy legislation of this country, despite the Acts of 1890 and 1891, remains in an unsettled state; and the care and treatment of the insane are burdened with vexations and unnecessary restrictions. Not only are the steps required for the placing of a person of unsound mind under legal care complicated and clumsy, but they result in many cases in a delay of that early treatment which is so important in cases of mental disease."

Dr. F. W. Mott writes :—

"There is yet one point which it is desirable to mention, as the result of both hospital and asylum experience, and that is the necessity of some earnest attempt being made to establish a means of intercepting, for hospital treatment, such cases of incipient and acute insanity as are not yet certifiable. It is probable that many would not come into the asylums, and a certain number of cases thus come under observation willingly, and in time to retard the progress of the disease. Practitioners could send doubtful cases for observation and treatment to such hospitals, where, moreover, the opportunity would be afforded of improving their own knowledge as to the early signs of insanity."[1]

He urges the desirability of the establishment of special wards in connection with general hospitals, pointing out that a mental case coming from such a ward would not thereby be stigmatised as insane. He quotes from 'an American writer on psychiatry ':—" Fortunate would be the community in which there was a fully equipped

[1] *Archives of Neurology*, 1903, Vol. II, p. 1.

and well-organised psychiatrical clinic under the control
of a university and dedicated to the solution of such
problems.   The mere existence of such an institution
would indicate that people were as much interested in
endeavouring to increase the public sanity as they are in
the results of exploration in the uttermost parts of the
earth, or in the discovery of a new star."[2]

The Medico-Psychological Association's report says :—

"The lunacy law does not permit of the establishment of
clinics on the lines which have been recommended, nor does
it provide for the admission of uncertified cases to the public
asylums.   This, for the present at any rate, renders nugatory
the suggested schemes for affording treatment for incipient and
non-confirmed cases of mental disorder, and with that, to a
large extent, fail the opportunities for study on which stress
has been laid for adding to the knowledge and increasing the
efficiency of asylum medical officers."   (p. 10.)

Such weighty opinions as these serve to emphasise a
further factor in the urgently needed reform—the necessity
for a thorough overhauling of the law of lunacy, so that,
while guarding the liberty of the subject, every obstacle
should be removed that obstructs patients threatened with
the dire calamity of insanity from securing preventive
treatment at the earliest possible moment.

In the *Lancet* of August 5th, 1916, Dr. L. A. Weatherley
writes :—

"The great fact that must be continually brought forward
in all these discussions is that, according to the reports of the
Commissioners in Lunacy, the *recovery-rate of mental diseases
is to-day no higher than it was in the 'seventies' of last
century.*   The ever-increasing difficulty in getting mental
cases with small means quickly under skilled care must, I feel
sure, account to a great extent for this lamentable fact."

"Marking time" since the seventies of the last century
—how does this condition compare with that of most of

---

[2] *Archives of Neurology,* 1907, Vol. III, p. 28.

the other branches of medical science? Heart disease,
diphtheria, tuberculosis, tetanus, sepsis of all kinds, all
these troubles and many others have shown unmistakable
signs of yielding to the incessant and many-sided assaults
of medical research. And, of insanity, all we have to
report in this country is "little or no progress for fifty
years." Verily we have buried our talent deep in the
ground.

Finally, we may quote from an article the opening
sentences of which might have been written yesterday,
Yet it was published in 1849! It was the fourth report
of the visiting committee of Hanwell Asylum. The committee say:—

"In the constitution of the Hanwell Asylum we are also
struck by the paucity of the medical officers attached to it.
There appear in round numbers to be about 500 patients on
the male and 500 on the female side, yet there is only one
resident medical officer attached to each department, and
one visiting physician for the whole establishment. The
inefficiency of so small a medical staff is obvious. If we look
across the Channel we find in Paris that the Salpêtrière,
with its thousand patients, has four times the number of
visiting physicians and ten times the number of resident
medical officers. The disproportion between the sane and the
insane is here so great that it is impossible under such a
system to bring any moral influence to bear upon the afflicted
multitude."

". . . There ought to be a more numerous medical staff
*and a permanent clinic* attached to such an institution. . . .
The County Asylum of Hanwell, supported largely as it is
by county rates and parish assessments, is as much a hospital
as St. George's or St. Bartholomew's, and ought to have a
medical staff as numerous and efficient as those of any other
metropolitan hospitals. While charity might thus be ad-
ministered upon the highest principles of Christian benevolence,
something ought to be done to advance our knowledge of
science and thereby enable us to relieve the afflictions of
suffering humanity."

The dust lies thick upon this volume, published a short
time before the *Crimean*, not the present war. And

to-day, like this early Victorian committee, we still ask
for clinics, we still ask for scientific work to be carried out
by a more numerous and better equipped staff, we still
look across the Channel with admiration—in short,
approving the better, we follow the worse. We have
dawdled away half-a-century and more in comparative
idleness. Now the war has taught us our lesson. Are
we to forget it again?

Excuses for inertia, brought forward before August,
1914, can be accepted no longer. The thousands of cases
of shell-shock which have been seen in our hospitals
since that time have proved, beyond any possibility of
doubt, that the early treatment of mental disorder is
successful from the humanitarian, medical and financial
standpoints. It is for us, not for our children, to act in
the light of this great lesson.

# Index.

*Printed by S. Clarke Limited, 41, Granby Row, Manchester.*

Printed in the United States
150191LV00011B/141/A

9 780548 900130